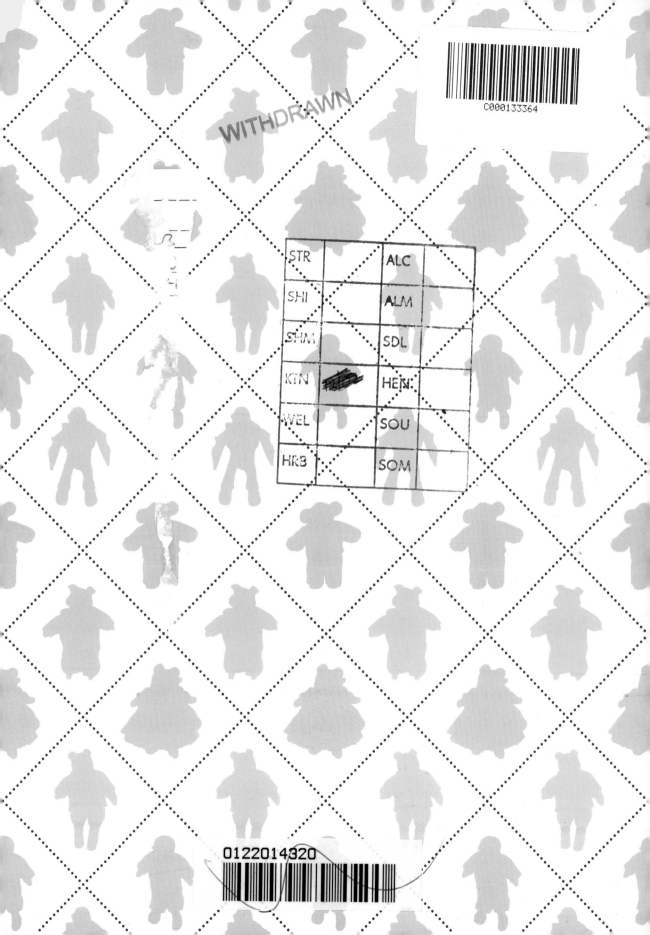

Making Soft-bodied
Dough Characters

Making Soft-bodied Dough Characters

Patricia Hughes

Guild of Master Craftsman Publications Ltd

First published 2000 by
Guild of Master Craftsman Publications Ltd,
166 High Street, Lewes,
East Sussex BN7 1XU

ISBN 1 86108 173 1

A catalogue record of this book is available from the British Library

Edited by Nicola Wright
Designed by Paul Griffin
Photographed by Anthony Bailey
Typeface: Stone Sans & Comic Sans
Colour separation: Viscan Graphics P.L. (Singapore)
Printed and bound by Kyodo Printing (Singapore)
under the supervision of
MRM Graphics, Winslow, Buckinghamshire, UK

10 9 8 7 6 5 4 3 2 1

I would like to dedicate this book to the memory of my mother, Roseanna Cruise

Contents

WARNING

These soft-bodied dough characters are ornaments and not toys. They should not be given to small children, as some contain small parts, which could be dangerous.

Introduction

After my first book on doughcraft had been published, I was eager to write another, but I wanted to find an aspect of the craft that had not been tackled before. After experimenting and searching for ideas for some time, I finally found a salt-dough figure whose head and limbs were made from salt dough while the body was made from fabric and stuffed with fibre filling. I was surprised to discover how easy it was to make, and all my friends wanted one. So I set about creating a selection of unique figures which, nevertheless, shared this same basic framework. I hope that you have as much fun making these characters, as I have had in developing them.

Tools and Materials

• • • • • • • • • • • •

You probably already have the basic tools and equipment needed to make and model dough in your kitchen: plain flour, table salt, water, a rolling pin and a small knife. As you experiment, you will find all sorts of implements and gadgets come in handy.

Basic equipment

Plain flour, table salt, water
Mixing bowl, rolling pin, fork to mix the dough
Non-stick baking tray
A variety of watercolour paints
Yacht varnish

Useful tools and materials

You will also need a variety of items to make up the dough characters:

A range of paintbrushes, for smoothing the dough, painting and varnishing

Cocktail sticks, for making holes in the dough, and supporting small pieces

Hairpins, for joining the head to the body of the figures

Wire cutters, for bending and cutting wire

Small black beads, for the eyes of figures

Garlic press, for making long strands of dough – ideal for hair

Gold wire, for accessories – i.e. halo for the angel and supporting roses etc.

Drinking straws, for making holes in the dough

Small sharp knife, for cutting the dough

Tweezers, for positioning small pieces of dough and pushing in stamens for whiskers

Needles

Cotton

Strong sewing thread, used double

Scissors

Glue, for sticking clothes and accessories

Pastry cutters, for creating hats and other accessories

Salt Dough

• • • • • • • • • • • •

The ingredients for salt dough are cheap and readily available

– flour, salt and water – so you can afford to experiment.

MAKING SALT DOUGH

1 Mix together the flour and salt in a mixing bowl. Add the water and bind the mixture together with a fork.

> ### You will need:
> • • • • • • • • • • • • • • • • • • •
> 225g (8oz) plain flour
> 100g (4oz) table salt
> 100ml (4fl oz or $\frac{1}{2}$ cup) water

2 Scoop the mixture into a ball with your hands and start to knead it. If the mixture feels too wet, add more flour; if it is too dry, add a little more water, a drop at a time (*see photo opposite*).

3 Knead the dough for 10–15 minutes. Poorly kneaded dough will crack when baked so it is worth making an effort at this stage to avoid disappointment later.

4 Once you have prepared the shapes you require, place them on a baking tray or ovenproof sheet.

5 Wrap any unused dough in cling film to prevent it drying out. If wrapped, it will stay fresh for about a day.

BAKING SALT DOUGH

Salt-dough models should be baked at temperatures of between 100–120°C (200–250°F or gas mark $1/4$–$1/2$). Any hotter than this and the dough will dry on the outside, but stay damp on the inside. All ovens vary, and as you become familiar with baking salt dough, you will find a suitable temperature for your oven. Each project in this book has a suggested baking time. The amount of time it takes to bake a salt-dough model will depend on the model's size and thickness. As a general guide, however, it takes approximately one hour per 6mm ($1/4$in) thickness of dough to bake. Test to see whether the dough is baked by giving it a gentle squeeze. If it feels soft, bake it for a little longer. If, on the other hand, you find that the dough is baking too quickly, move it to a lower shelf in the oven and reduce the temperature slightly.

It is worth remembering that, unless they are washed immediately after use, metal objects, like cutters and uncoated baking trays, will tend to rust because of the salt in the dough.

PROBLEMS

CRACKING

Your dough may crack for one of a number of reasons. Most commonly, either your dough has not been kneaded sufficiently, or it has been baked at too high a temperature. If the oven is too hot, the dough will swell on the inside, causing it to crack. Rapid temperature changes are a potential risk too, so, to be on the safe side, give the dough time to adjust to a cooler temperature by leaving it to cool down gradually in the oven when you have turned off the heat. Sometimes cracks will appear some hours after the dough has been baked. If this happens, just fill in the cracks with some fresh dough, but rather than returning the dough to the oven for further baking, leave it to air-dry for a few hours. When the dough is completely dry, sand the filled cracks smooth with fine sandpaper.

WETNESS

A salt-dough model that has been kept in a damp atmosphere will almost certainly have absorbed some of the moisture and become wet. To test whether the dough is wet, give it a gentle squeeze to see if it feels soft and pliable. If the model is wet, place it in a warm, dry place, like an airing cupboard, and leave it to dry out for a few days.

FINISHING

PAINTING

You can use many different types of paint to colour your dough.

Poster paints: produce bright colours, but can dry powdery.

Watercolours: come in conveniently small tubes and are easy to use.

Gouache: is also sold in small tubes. The fact that it can either be used neat to make an opaque block of colour, or watered down to give a gentle wash makes it a versatile and attractive option.

Humbrol: is spirit-based paint, but can, like gouache, be used in either a concentrated or dilute form. Remember, though, that because it is not water-based, it has to be thinned with white spirit (mineral spirit).

VARNISHING

It is essential to apply at least two coats of clear gloss oil-based polyurethane varnish to your salt-dough models because as a medium, the dough is extremely vulnerable to moisture. Yacht varnish, which is available from DIY stores, is a good, strong sealant. Make sure you cover any small nooks and crannies. It is a good idea to keep one brush solely for

varnishing, remembering always to clean it afterwards in white spirit, turpentine or a turpentine substitute – otherwise it will go hard.

EGG GLAZING

An alternative to painting your dough model is glazing it with egg. This will give you a lovely golden brown finish. Beat an egg with one tablespoon of water, and brush it onto the raw dough before baking. Apply a fresh layer every half hour whilst the dough is being baked.

JOINING SALT DOUGH

Wet one surface of the join with a little water using a small paintbrush (*see photo above*). Too much water will make the dough slide around, making it difficult to join. Gently push the two pieces together, and leave to dry.

LOOPS – USING HAIRPINS

You will need a straight, strong hairpin to secure the head to the body. Having first cut down the rounded end of the hairpin with wire cutters to 25mm (1in), push half of its length 13mm ($\frac{1}{2}$in) into the head under the chin, leaving visible the remaining 13mm ($\frac{1}{2}$in).

Techniques

• • • • • • • • • • • •

There are a few basic techniques that you need to master in
order to make the soft-bodied dough characters.

MAKING A HEAD BASE

If you lay the head of your dough model
face up on the baking tray, it will flatten it at
the back. To prevent this you will need to
make a base for the head so that it can
stand upright whilst baking. (If your model
is going to wear a hat, however, you will
not need a head base.) Once you have
made the base, you can use it to support
the heads of all your models. As a rule, salt
dough should always be varnished to
protect it from moisture, but you will not be
able to varnish the head base, because it

will be used in the oven, and the heat
would make it smell very unpleasant. When
you are not using the base, store it in an
airtight container.

> **You will need:**
> • • • • • • • • • • • • •
>
> 25g (1oz) plain flour
> 13g (½oz) table salt
> 13ml (½fl oz or ⅟₁₆ cup) water
> Small sharp knife
> Kitchen foil

1 Once you have made and kneaded the dough, roll it into a ball and place it on a work surface.

2 Cut off the top piece with the knife as if it were a boiled egg (*see photo page 9*).

3 Turn the ball upside down and cut off the opposite end.

4 With the point of the knife, make a slit across the centre of the top about 13mm ($\frac{1}{2}$in) wide and 13mm ($\frac{1}{2}$in) deep.

5 Fold up some kitchen foil into a 13mm ($\frac{1}{2}$in) square. Push this into the slit you have made; it will prevent the two sides sticking together while the base is baking.

6 Place the head base on a baking tray and bake at 120°C (250°F or gas mark $\frac{1}{2}$) for two hours.

7 Allow to cool, and then remove the foil.

MAKING A SOFT BODY

You will need:

Needle and thread
19.5 x 7.5cm ($7\frac{3}{4}$ x 3in)
White cotton fabric
Fibre filling, to stuff the body

1 Place the fabric lengthways in front of you and with right sides together, fold it in half top to bottom. With a seam allowance of 6mm ($\frac{1}{4}$in), stitch up the two sides.

2 Turn the fabric so that it is right side out, and stuff the body quite firmly with the fibre filling (*see photo below*). The fold of the fabric is at the bottom and the top is left open.

3 Stitch from the top corners across the top opening to form the shoulder seams, leaving a gap 13mm (¹/₂in) wide in the centre of the body.

ASSEMBLING THE HEAD, BODY, ARMS AND LEGS

You will need:

Darning needle

Strong button thread

Fast-setting glue

1 Using double thread, sew the arms and legs to the body, finishing off with a few firm stitches.

2 Using double thread again, make a few stitches one on top of the other in the centre back of the body (do not cast off).

3 Push the needle into the back of the body, and bring it up through the opening at the top (*see photo above*). Thread the needle through the hole of the hairpin at the bottom of the head and, keeping the thread loose, push it back down into the neck opening and out through the centre back of the body.

4 Put a few drops of fast-setting glue around the prongs of the hairpin under the head and then pull tight the thread at the back of the body, bringing the head and body firmly together. Hold the thread tight for 30 seconds. The head should now be firmly attached to the body. Make a few casting-off stitches and cut the thread.

Mother Rabbit and Babies

Someone you know would love
this charming Mother Rabbit and
babies. Alternatively, you could
make the Mother Teddy Bear,
Mrs Mouse or Mrs Hedgehog.

Actual size: height 15cm (6in)

Salt dough

75g (3oz) plain flour

40g (1$\frac{1}{2}$oz) table salt

40ml (1$\frac{1}{2}$fl oz or $\frac{3}{16}$cup) water

In addition to your basic tools and equipment you will need:

Small sharp knife

Small paintbrush

3 cocktail sticks

2 small black beads for the eyes

Drinking straw (medium-hole)

Hairpin, cut to 25mm (1in)

Fast-setting glue

Paints: black, light brown and pink

66 x 10cm (26 x 4in) fabric for the dress

51cm (20in) lace 6mm ($\frac{1}{4}$in) wide

12.5 x 12.5cm (5 x 5in) fabric for the hat

25.5 x 10cm (10 x 4in) fabric for the knickers

15 x 10cm (6 x 4in) fabric for the apron

25.5cm (10in) ribbon 6mm ($\frac{1}{4}$in) wide

Small pieces of pink and blue fabric and small amount of fibre filling
to make the babies' beds

TO MAKE THE MOTHER RABBIT'S HEAD, ARMS, LEGS AND BABIES

1 Roll a ball of dough the size of a golf ball. Roll out another piece of dough thinly, cut a tiny triangle for the nose, and fix it to the head. Roll two tiny ropes of dough for the cheeks and join them either side of the nose, leaving a small gap in the centre for the whisker parts. Smooth around the cheeks with a damp paintbrush (*see photo opposite*).

2 To make the whisker parts, roll two pea-sized balls of dough and flatten them slightly. Fix these between the cheeks and make some small holes with the point of a cocktail stick to suggest whiskers.

3 To make the eyes, mark out two circles on the head with the knife. Push the knife in a little further all the way around

Step 1 (page 14) Smoothing the cheeks

the circle, and lift out the surface layer of the dough. Paint each eyehole with a wet paintbrush, and press a bead into each of the holes.

4 Make the ears from two flattened ropes of dough. Curl them slightly together, and join them to the head.

5 Push the hairpin into the lower part of the head under the chin to a depth of 13mm ($\frac{1}{2}$in).

6 To make the arms, roll a finger-sized rope of dough about 7.5cm (3in) long. Cut the rope in half and round off one end of each piece with your finger and thumb. At the shoulder end, make a hole 6mm ($\frac{1}{4}$in) from the top, with a drinking straw.

7 To make the legs, roll another rope of dough 10cm (4in) long. Cut it in half

and round off one end of each piece. To create the hip joint, make a hole with a drinking straw 6mm ($\frac{1}{4}$in) from the other end.

8 To make the babies, start by rolling five marble-sized balls of dough for the heads. Then break cocktail sticks into five 25mm (1in) lengths and push one into each head to a depth of 13mm ($\frac{1}{2}$in).

9 Make holes for the babies' eyes with the point of a cocktail stick (*see photo overleaf*). Roll five tiny balls of dough for the noses, and ten tiny ropes for the ears. Fix these to the babies' heads.

10 Place all the pieces on a baking tray and bake at 100°C (200°F or gas mark $\frac{1}{4}$) for about five hours.

Step 9 (page 15) Making the babies' eyes

11 When the dough has cooled, secure the hairpin in the mother's head and the cocktail sticks in the babies' heads with a little fast-setting glue. Make hanging loops for each piece by threading some sewing cotton through the loop of the hairpin and through the holes in the arms and legs and tying it off.

12 When the baked dough is cool, you can paint it. Use black for both the mother's and her babies' eyes. Then paint the mother's nose and the noses and ears of the babies pink and the mother's whisker parts brown.

13 Apply two coats of varnish to all the dough parts.

14 To make the soft body, and to attach the head, arms and legs, see Techniques pages 10–11.

MAKING THE MOTHER RABBIT'S CLOTHES

DRESS

1 Using tracing paper, make copies of pattern nos. 2 and 3 (see pages 135–136).

2 Pin pattern no. 2 to a double layer of fabric and cut out. Stitch the two pieces together along the shoulder, side and underarm seams with a 6mm ($1/4$in) seam allowance.

3 Fold the bodice in half, side seams together and crease. Unfold again and carefully cut straight up the foldline at the centre of the back of the bodice from the waist to the neckline; this will form the centre-back seam of the dress.

4 Using a double thickness of fabric, cut out pattern no. 3 for the skirt. Run a gathering stitch across the top and, with right sides together, join the top of the dress to the skirt at the waist.

5 Turn up a 6mm (¹⁄₄in) hem at the bottom of the dress. Stitch.

6 With right sides together, stitch the centre-back seam of the dress, leaving a 5cm (2in) opening at the top.

7 Put the dress on the rabbit, and slip stitch to close the opening at the back.

8 Stitch some lace around the sleeves with small running stitches, and pull the stitches to gather the sleeves around the arms.

Step 5 (page 18) Making the apron with pockets

KNICKERS

1 Using tracing paper, make a copy of pattern no. 5 (see page 138).

2 Cut it out twice in fabric, and with right sides together, stitch the side and inner leg seams, with a 6mm (¹⁄₄in) seam allowance.

3 Stitch some lace around the bottom with small running stitches and pull the stitches to gather them around the legs.

HAT

1 Using tracing paper, make a copy of pattern no. 6 (see page 136).

2 Cut out the shape from a single thickness of fabric. Cut two holes for the rabbit's ears as indicated.

3 Stitch some lace around the outside edge, and fit the hat around the rabbit's head by gathering the stitches.

APRON WITH POCKETS

1 Using tracing paper, make a copy of pattern no. 4 (see page 137).

2 Cut out the shape from a single thickness of fabric. Turn and stitch a 6mm ($1/4$in) hem at two sides.

3 Turn up a 25mm (1in) hem at the bottom and press. Then turn under 6mm ($1/4$in) at the raw edge of the turn-up.

4 Divide the hem into five equal-sized pockets and stitch them in place.

5 Run a gathering thread across the top of the apron and adjust the gathers until the waist of the apron measures 7.5cm (3in) (see photo on page 17).

Step 1 Making the babies' beds

6 Making sure that you leave the ends long enough to tie a bow at the back, sew the ribbon across the gathered top of the apron.

TO MAKE THE BABIES' BEDS

1 Apply a little fast-setting glue around the cocktail stick sticking out of each baby's head and wrap a small amount of fibre filling around it to make a body (see photo below).

2 Cut the pink and blue fabric into five rectangles, each measuring 5 x 2.5cm (2 x 1in). Fold the rectangles in half, and sew up the sides with a 6mm ($1/4$in) seam allowance.

3 Slip the babies into their fabric beds. Put the babies into the apron pockets.

4 Finally, tie the filled apron around the mother rabbit's waist.

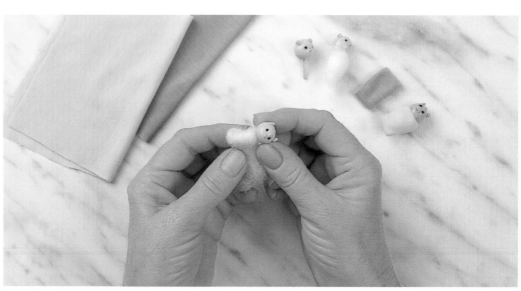

If you enjoyed making the mother rabbit

and babies, why not try this

Mother Teddy Bear with Babies

Actual size: height 15cm (6in)

TO MAKE THE MOTHER TEDDY'S HEAD, ARMS, LEGS AND BABIES

1 Roll a ball of dough the size of a golf ball for the mother teddy's head. Roll a small ball for the nose and join it to the head. Smooth around the join with a damp paintbrush. Roll out another piece of dough thinly, cut a small triangle, and join it to the end of the nose. Make holes for the eyes with the point of a cocktail stick. Wet these holes and push a bead into each eye socket.

Salt dough

75g (3oz) plain flour

40g (1½oz) table salt

40ml (1½fl oz or ³⁄₁₆ cup) water

In addition to your basic tools and equipment you will need:

3 cocktail sticks

2 small black beads for the eyes

1 hairpin cut to 25mm (1in)

Ready-made head base (see Techniques page 9)

Small sharp knife

Drinking straw (medium-hole)

Fast-setting glue

Black paint

66 x 10cm (26 x 4in) fabric for the dress

23cm (9in) lace 6mm (¼in) wide

25.5 x 10cm (10 x 4in) fabric for the knickers

12.5 x 5cm (5 x 2in) fabric for the head scarf

15 x 10cm (6 x 4in) fabric for the apron

25.5cm (10in) ribbon 6mm (¼in) wide

Small pieces of pink and blue fabric and small amount of fibre filling

to make the babies' beds

2 Make the ears from two small flattened balls of dough, and join them to the head. Push the hairpin into the lower part of the head under the chin to a depth of 13mm (½in), and position it in the head base with the rounded end of the hairpin in the centre opening.

3 To make the arms, roll a finger-sized rope of dough about 7.5cm (3in) long. Cut the rope in half and round off one end of each piece with your finger and thumb. Using a drinking straw, make a hole 6mm (¼in) from the other end of the arm – at the shoulder.

4 To make the legs, roll another rope of dough 10cm (4in) long but slightly fatter than the arms. Cut it in half, round off one end of each piece, turning the feet slightly upwards. Make a hole 6mm (¼in) from the tops of the legs with a straw.

5 To make the babies, start by rolling five marble-sized balls of dough for the heads. Break the cocktail sticks into five 25mm (1in) lengths, and push one into each head to a depth of 13mm ($\frac{1}{2}$in).

6 Make holes for the babies' eyes with the point of a cocktail stick. Roll five tiny balls of dough for the noses, and ten tiny flattened balls for the ears. Fix these to the heads.

7 Place the head in the head base and all these pieces onto a baking tray and bake at 100°C (200°F or gas mark $\frac{1}{4}$) for about five hours.

8 When the dough has cooled, secure the hairpin in the mother's head and the cocktail sticks in the babies' heads with a little fast-setting glue. Make hanging loops for each piece by threading some sewing cotton through the loop of the hairpin and through the holes in the arms and legs and tying it off.

9 When the baked dough is cool, paint the mother's nose and the babies' eyes black, and the babies' noses and ears pink.

10 Apply two coats of varnish.

11 To make the mother teddy's soft body, and to attach the head, arms and legs, see Techniques pages 10–11.

MAKING THE MOTHER TEDDY'S CLOTHES

DRESS

1 Using tracing paper, make copies of pattern nos. 2 and 3 (see pages 135–136).

2 Pin pattern no. 2 to a double layer of fabric and cut out. Stitch the two pieces together along the shoulder, side and underarm seams with a 6mm ($\frac{1}{4}$in) seam allowance.

3 Fold the bodice in half, side seams together and crease. Unfold again and carefully cut straight up the foldline at the centre of the back of the bodice from the waist to the neckline; this will form the centre-back seam of the dress.

4 Using a double thickness of fabric, cut out pattern no. 3 for the skirt. Run a gathering stitch across the top and, with right sides together, join the top of the dress to the skirt at the waist.

5 Turn up a 6mm ($\frac{1}{4}$in) hem at the bottom of the dress. Stitch.

6 With right sides together, stitch the centre-back seam of the dress, leaving a 5cm (2in) opening at the top.

7 Put the dress on the teddy bear, and slip stitch to close the opening at the back of the dress.

8 Stitch some lace around the sleeves with small running stitches, and pull the stitches to gather the sleeves around the arms.

KNICKERS

1 Using tracing paper, make a copy of pattern no. 5 (see page 138).

2 Cut it out twice in fabric, and with right sides together, stitch the side and inner leg seams, with a 6mm (¼in) seam allowance.

3 Stitch some lace around the bottom of each leg with small running stitches and gather the stitches to fit them around the legs.

HEADSCARF

Fold the piece of fabric in half lengthways, and tie it around the teddy's head.

APRON WITH POCKETS

1 Using tracing paper, make a copy of pattern no. 4 (see page 137).

2 Cut out the shape from a single thickness of fabric. Turn and stitch a 6mm (¼in) hem at two sides.

3 Turn up a 25mm (1in) hem at the bottom and press. Then turn under 6mm (¼in) at the raw edge of the turn-up and press.

4 Divide the hem into five equal-sized pockets and stitch them in place.

5 Run a gathering thread across the top of the apron and adjust the gathers until the waist of the apron measures 7.5cm (3in).

6 Making sure that you leave the ends long enough to tie a bow at the back, sew the ribbon across the gathered top of the apron.

TO MAKE THE BABIES' BEDS

1 Apply a little fast-setting glue to the cocktail stick sticking out of each baby's head and wrap a small amount of fibre filling around it to make a body.

2 Cut the pink and blue fabric into five rectangles, each measuring 5 x 2.5cm (2 x 1in). Fold the rectangles in half, and sew up the sides with a 6mm (¼in) seam allowance.

3 Slip the babies into their pink and blue fabric beds.

4 Place the babies in the apron pockets.

5 Finally, tie the filled apron around the mother teddy's waist.

Alternatively

A spritely, pretty character, **Mrs Mouse** can be easily made following similar steps to the Mother Rabbit and Mother Teddy Bear.

Actual size: height 15cm (6in)

MAKING THE HEAD, ARMS AND LEGS

1 Roll a ball of dough the size of a golf ball, and pinch out one piece for the nose. Make a hole at the end of the nose with a cocktail stick. Wet the hole and push in a black bead.

2 Use the cocktail stick to make holes for the eyes, wet the holes, and push a black bead into each socket.

Salt dough

Salt dough

50g (2oz) plain flour

25g (1oz) table salt

25ml (1 fl oz or $\frac{1}{8}$ cup) water

In addition to your basic tools and equipment you will need:

1 hairpin cut to 25mm (1in)

Cocktail stick

3 small black beads for the eyes and nose

2 black stamens for the whiskers (available from craft shops)

Small sharp knife

Drinking straw (medium-hole)

Fast-setting glue

Pink paint

66 x 10cm (26 x 4in) fabric to make the dress

30cm (12in) lace 6mm ($\frac{1}{4}$in) wide

12.5 x 12.5cm (5 x 5in) fabric to make the hat

25 x 10cm (10 x 4in) fabric to make the knickers

15 x 14cm (6 x $5\frac{1}{2}$in) fabric to make the apron

25.5cm (10in) ribbon 6mm ($\frac{1}{4}$in) wide

3 Make the ears from two small, flattened balls of dough, curl them slightly and fix them to the head.

4 Cut the stamens into six equal lengths. Push the ends into either side of the nose to act as whiskers.

5 Push the hairpin into the lower part of the head under the chin to a depth of 13mm ($\frac{1}{2}$in).

6 To make the arms, roll a finger-sized rope of dough about 7.5cm (3in) long. Cut the rope in half and round off one end of each arm with your finger and thumb. Using a drinking straw, make a hole 6mm ($\frac{1}{4}$in) from the other end of the arm – at the shoulder.

7 To make the legs, roll another rope 10cm (4in) long. Cut it in half and round off the ends. Turn up ends for the slippers. Roll a thin rope and join a piece around the ankles. Roll two tiny balls of dough and join them to the slippers for the pom-poms. Make a hole 6mm ($\frac{1}{4}$in) from the tops of the legs with a drinking straw.

8 Place the head, arms and legs onto a baking tray and bake at 100°C (200°F or gas mark $\frac{1}{4}$) for about five hours.

9 When the dough has cooled put some fast-setting glue around the holes of the hairpin, to keep it in place.

10 Thread some sewing cotton through the hole of the hairpin and

holes in the arms and legs and tie it off to make hanging loops for each piece.

11 When the baked dough is cool, paint the inside of the mouse's ears and the slippers pink.

12 Apply two coats of varnish.

13 To make the soft body, and to attach the head, arms and legs, see Techniques pages 10–11.

MAKING THE MOUSE'S CLOTHES

DRESS

1 Using tracing paper, make copies of pattern nos. 2 and 3 (see pages 135–136).

2 Pin pattern no. 2 to a double layer of fabric and cut out. Stitch the two pieces together along the shoulder, side and underarm seams with a 6mm ($1/4$in) seam allowance.

3 Fold the bodice in half, side seams together and crease. Unfold again and carefully cut straight up the foldline at the centre of the back of the bodice from the waist to the neckline; this will form the centre-back seam of the dress.

4 Using a double thickness of fabric, cut out pattern no. 3 for the skirt. Run a gathering stitch across the top and, with right sides together, join the top of the dress to the skirt at the waist.

5 Turn up a 6mm ($1/4$in) hem at the bottom of the dress. Stitch.

6 With right sides together, stitch the centre-back seam of the dress, leaving a 5cm (2in) opening at the top.

7 Put the dress on the mouse, and slip stitch closed the opening at the back.

8 Stitch some lace around the sleeves with small running stitches, and pull the stitches to gather the sleeves around the arms. For instructions on how to make the apron, see page 29.

KNICKERS

1 Using tracing paper, make a copy of pattern no. 5 (see page 138).

2 Cut it out twice in fabric, and with right sides together, stitch the side and inner leg seams, with a 6mm ($1/4$in) seam allowance.

3 Stitch some lace around the bottom with small running stitches and pull the stitches to gather them around the legs.

HAT

1 Using tracing paper, make a copy of pattern no. 6 (see page 134).

2 Cut out the shape from a single thickness of fabric. Cut two holes for the mouse's ears as indicated.

3 Stitch some lace around the outside edge, and fit the hat around the mouse's head by gathering the stitches.

Alternatively

If you enjoyed making Mrs Mouse, why not try making cheerful **Mrs Hedgehog** with her pretty dress and apron.

Actual size: height 15cm (6in)

MAKING THE HEAD, ARMS AND LEGS

1 Roll a ball of dough the size of a golf ball, pinch out a small part for the nose, and turn it slightly upwards.

2 Roll two pea-sized balls of dough for the cheeks, and attach them either side of the nose. Smooth around the edges of the cheeks with a damp paintbrush.

Salt dough

75g (3oz) plain flour

40g (1$\frac{1}{2}$oz) table salt

40ml (1$\frac{1}{2}$fl oz or $\frac{3}{16}$ cup) water

In addition to your basic tools and equipment you will need:

Garlic press

Cocktail stick

1 hairpin cut to 25mm (1in)

Small sharp knife

Drinking straw (medium-hole)

Ready-made head base (see Techniques page 9)

Fast-setting glue

Paints: black, brown and red

66 x 10cm (26 x 4in) fabric to make the dress

25.5 x 10cm (10 x 4in) fabric to make the knickers

15 x 14cm (6 x 5$\frac{1}{2}$in) fabric to make the apron

30cm (12in) lace 6mm ($\frac{1}{4}$in) wide

25.5cm (10in) ribbon 6mm ($\frac{1}{4}$in) wide

91.5cm (1yd) narrow ribbon for the cuffs and ankles

3 Push some dough through a garlic press to make hair.

4 Join the hair to the head, starting at the nose and working your way around until the entire head is covered with the strands of dough.

5 Make the holes for the eyes with a cocktail stick.

6 Roll a tiny ball for the nose, and join it to the head.

7 Make two tiny ears, from flattened balls of dough, and join them to the head.

8 Push the hairpin into the lower part of the head under the chin to a depth of 13mm ($\frac{1}{2}$in).

9 To make the arms, roll a finger-sized rope of dough about 7.5cm (3in) long. Cut the rope in half and round off one end of each arm with your finger and thumb. Using a drinking straw, make a hole 6mm ($\frac{1}{4}$in) from the other end of the arm – at the shoulder.

10 To make the legs, roll another rope 10cm (4in) long. Cut it in half and round off the ends. Make a hole 6mm ($\frac{1}{4}$in) from the tops of the legs with a drinking straw.

11 Position the head in the head base, and place with the arms and legs onto a baking tray. Bake at 100°C (200°F or gas mark $\frac{1}{4}$) for about five hours.

12 When the dough has cooled, put some fast-setting glue around the holes of the hairpin, to keep it in place.

13 Thread some sewing cotton through the loop of the hairpin and the holes in the arms and legs and tie it off to make hanging loops for each piece.

14 When the baked dough is cool, paint the hair brown; the nose black and the cheeks watery red.

15 Apply two coats of varnish.

16 To make the soft body, and to attach the head, arms and legs, see Techniques pages 10–11.

MAKING THE HEDGEHOG'S CLOTHES

DRESS

1 Using tracing paper, make copies of pattern nos. 2 and 3 (see pages 135–136).

2 Pin pattern no. 2 to a double layer of fabric and cut out. Stitch the two pieces together along the shoulder, side and underarm seams with a 6mm ($\frac{1}{4}$in) seam allowance.

3 Fold the bodice in half, side seams together and crease. Unfold again and carefully cut straight up the foldline at the centre of the back of the bodice from the waist to the neckline; this will form the centre-back seam of the dress.

4 Using a double thickness of fabric, cut out pattern no. 3 for the skirt. Run a gathering stitch across the top and, with right sides together, join the top of the dress to the skirt at the waist.

5 Turn up a 6mm ($\frac{1}{4}$in) hem at the bottom of the dress. Stitch.

6 With right sides together, stitch the centre-back seam of the dress, leaving a 5cm (2in) opening at the top.

7 Put the dress on the hedgehog, and slip stitch closed the opening at the back of the dress.

8 Stitch some lace around the sleeves with small running stitches, and pull the stitches to gather the sleeves around the arms.

KNICKERS

1 Using tracing paper, make a copy of pattern no. 5 (see page 138).

2 Cut it out twice in fabric, and with right sides together, stitch the side and inner leg seams, with a 6mm (1/4in) seam allowance.

3 Stitch some lace around the bottom with small running stitches and pull the stitches to gather them around the legs.

APRON

1 Using tracing paper, make a copy of pattern no. 4 (see page 137).

2 Cut out the shape from a single thickness of fabric. Turn and stitch a 6mm (1/4in) hem at the two sides and across the bottom.

3 Run a gathering thread across the top of the apron and adjust the gathers until the waist of the apron measures 7.5cm (3in).

4 Cut a piece of fabric 4 x 4cm (1 1/2 x 1 1/2in) for the bib of the apron. Turn and stitch a 6mm (1/4in) hem on three sides and then, with right sides together and centres matching, stitch together the two pieces of the apron.

5 To finish the apron, stitch the ribbon to the gathered edge, making sure that you leave the ends long enough to tie a bow at the back.

Daisy Doll

· · · · · · · · · · · ·

Little girls will love to own
this appealing doll with her
plaited hair, mop cap and
frilly knickers.

Actual size: height 15cm (6in)

Salt dough

50g (2oz) plain flour
25g (1oz) table salt
25ml (1fl oz or $\frac{1}{8}$ cup) water

In addition to your basic tools and equipment you will need:

1 hairpin cut to 25mm (1in)
Small sharp knife
Drinking straw (medium-hole)
Fast-setting glue
Paints: black, red, pink and blue
Small amount of orange wool for the hair
66 x 10cm (26 x 4in) fabric for the dress
40.5cm (16in) contrasting trim for the dress (optional)
51cm (20in) lace 6mm ($\frac{1}{4}$in) wide
25.5 x 10cm (10 x 4in) fabric for the knickers
12.5 x 12.5cm (5 x 5in) fabric for the hat
20cm (8in) ribbon 6mm ($\frac{1}{4}$in) wide

MAKING THE HEAD, ARMS AND LEGS

1 Roll a ball of dough the size of a table tennis ball for the head. Roll a tiny ball for the nose, and join it to the head. Push the hairpin into the lower part of the head under the chin to a depth of 13mm ($\frac{1}{2}$in), and place it onto a baking tray.

2 To make the arms, roll a finger-sized rope of dough about 7.5cm (3in) long. Cut the rope in half and round off one end of each arm with your finger and thumb. Flatten the rounded ends to make the hands. Cut a notch for the thumbs with a knife. Using a drinking straw, make a hole 6mm ($\frac{1}{4}$in) from the other end of the arm.

3 To make the legs, roll another slightly thicker rope 10cm (4in) long. Cut the rope in half. Roll two small marble-sized balls of dough for the shoes, and press your finger into the centre of each shoe to make a hole (see photo opposite). Join them to the ends of the legs. Roll two tiny balls of dough and attach them to the front of the shoes. Make a hole 6mm ($\frac{1}{4}$in) from the top of each leg with a drinking straw.

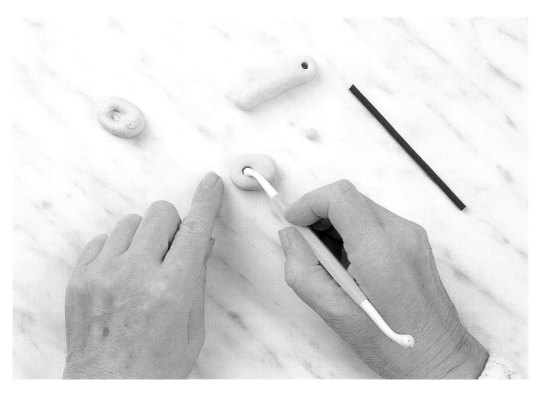

Step 3 (page 32) Making the doll's shoes

4 Place the arms and legs onto the baking tray with the head, and bake at 120°C (240°F or gas mark $^1/_2$) for about three hours.

5 When the dough has cooled put some fast-setting glue around the holes of the hairpin, to keep it in place.

6 Thread some sewing cotton through the hole of the hairpin and the holes in the arms and legs and tie it off to make hanging loops for each piece.

7 When the dough is cool, hang up the head, arms and legs so they are easier to paint and varnish.

8 Paint the eyes black; mix red and white to make pink for the cheeks and mouth; and paint the shoes blue. Apply two coats of varnish to the head, arms and legs.

9 Cut the orange wool into short lengths and glue it to the head, starting at the centre. Plait the hair into braids and tie them off with ribbon.

10 To make the soft body, and to attach the head, arms and legs, see Techniques pages 10–11.

MAKING THE DOLL'S CLOTHES

DRESS

1 Using tracing paper, make copies of pattern nos. 2 and 3 (see pages 135–136).

2 Pin pattern no. 2 to a double layer of fabric and cut out. Stitch the two pieces together along the shoulder, side and underarm seams with a 6mm (¼in) seam allowance.

3 Fold the bodice in half, side seams together and crease. Unfold again and carefully cut straight up the foldline at the centre of the back of the bodice from the waist to the neckline; this will form the centre-back seam of the dress.

4 Using a double thickness of fabric, cut out pattern no. 3 for the skirt. Run a gathering stitch across the top and, with right sides together, join the top of the dress to the skirt at the waist.

5 Turn up a 6mm (¼in) hem at the bottom of the dress. Stitch.

6 With right sides together, stitch the centre-back seam of the dress, leaving a 5cm (2in) opening at the top.

7 Sew the contrasting trim to the skirt of the dress.

8 Put the dress on the doll, and slip stitch closed the opening at the back.

9 Stitch some lace around the sleeves with small running stitches, and pull the stitches to gather the sleeves around the arms.

10 Tie the ribbon around the waist and make a bow at the back.

KNICKERS

1 Using tracing paper, make a copy of pattern no. 5 (see page 138).

2 Cut it out twice in fabric, and with right sides together, stitch the side and inner leg seams, with a 6mm (¼in) seam allowance.

3 Stitch some lace around the bottom with small running stitches and pull the stitches to gather them around the legs.

HAT

1 Using tracing paper, make a copy of pattern no. 6 (see page 134).

2 Cut out the shape from a single thickness of fabric.

3 Stitch some lace around the outside edge, and fit the hat around the doll's head by gathering the stitches.

Digger Mole

Someone you know would simply love this cute mole. By adapting the basic design you could also make an elephant and a teddy bear. The mole itself is simply shaped from salt dough with jacket and trousers added.

Actual size: height 15cm (6in)

Salt dough

50g (2oz) plain flour

25g (1oz) table salt

25ml (1fl oz or $\frac{1}{8}$ cup) water

In addition to your basic tools and equipment you will need:

Cocktail stick

3 small black beads for the eyes and nose

3 small pearl beads for the jacket

1 hairpin cut to 25mm (1in)

Ready-made head base (see page 9)

Small sharp knife

Drinking straw (medium-hole)

Fast-setting glue

Brown paint

30 x 7.5cm (12 x 3in) fabric for the jacket

23 x 7.5cm (9 x 3in) fabric for the trousers

TO MAKE THE HEAD, ARMS AND LEGS

1 Roll a ball of dough the size of a golf ball for the head. Pinch out a small piece for the nose, and turn it upwards slightly (*see photo below*). Make a hole at the end of the nose with a cocktail stick. Make holes for the eyes in the same way, wet the holes and push a bead into each eye socket and into the end of the nose.

Step 1 Shaping the mole's nose

2 Push the hairpin into the lower part of the head under the chin to a depth of 13mm ($\frac{1}{2}$in), and place the head onto the head base with the rounded end of the hairpin in the centre opening.

3 To make the arms, roll a small rope of dough about 7.5cm (3in) long. Cut the rope in half and round off one end of each arm with your finger and thumb. Using a drinking straw, make a hole 6mm ($\frac{1}{4}$in) from the other end of the arm.

4 To make the legs, roll another rope 10cm (4in) long. Cut the rope in half, and round off one end of each piece with your finger and thumb. Make a hole 6mm ($\frac{1}{4}$in) from the tops of the legs with the drinking straw.

5 Place the head on its head base, together with the arms and legs, onto a baking tray, and bake at 100°C (200°F or gas mark $\frac{1}{4}$) for about five hours.

6 When the dough has cooled put some fast-setting glue around the holes of the hairpin, to keep it in place.

7 Thread some sewing cotton through the hole of the hairpin and the holes in the arms and legs and tie it off to make hanging loops for each piece.

8 When the baked dough is cool, paint the head and limbs brown.

9 Apply two coats of varnish.

10 To make the mole's soft body, and to attach the head, arms and legs, see Techniques pages 10–11.

MAKING THE MOLE'S CLOTHES

JACKET

1 Using tracing paper, make a copy of pattern no. 7 (see page 139).

2 Pin pattern to a double layer of fabric and cut out. With right sides facing, stitch the two pieces together along the shoulder, side and underarm seams with a 6mm ($\frac{1}{4}$in) seam allowance.

3 Fold the bodice in half, side seams together and crease. Unfold again and carefully cut straight up the foldline at the centre of the front of the jacket from the waist to the neckline.

4 Put the jacket on the mole, stitch up the front and stitch beads for buttons.

TROUSERS

1 Using tracing paper, make a copy of pattern no. 8 (see page 139).

2 Pin pattern to a double layer of fabric and cut out. With right sides together, and with a seam allowance of 6mm ($\frac{1}{4}$in), sew the two pieces together – up both sides and along the inner leg seams.

3 Put the trousers onto the mole and secure with a couple of stitches through to the body.

Alternatively

If you enjoyed making the mole, why not try this **Edwin the Elephant** who differs from it only in the way the head is shaped.

Actual size: height 15cm (6in)

MAKING THE HEAD, ARMS AND LEGS

1 Roll a ball of dough the size of a golf ball for the head. Roll a finger-thick rope of dough for the trunk, and join it to the head turning the trunk upwards.

2 Make the ears from two flattened balls of dough. Cut a straight edge on each ear, and attach them to the head.

Salt dough

75g (3oz) plain flour

40g (1$\frac{1}{2}$oz) table salt

40ml (1$\frac{1}{2}$fl ozor $\frac{3}{16}$ cup) water

In addition to your basic tools and equipment you will need:

Small sharp knife

Cocktail stick

2 small black beads for the eyes and 2 small beads for the jacket

1 hairpin cut to 25mm (1in)

Ready-made head base (see Techniques page 9)

Drinking straw (medium hole)

Fast-setting glue

Paints: light grey and pink

30 x 7.5cm (12 x 3in) fabric for the jacket

23 x 7.5cm (9 x 3in) fabric for the trousers

3 Make holes for the eyes with a cocktail stick. Wet these holes and push a bead into each eye socket.

4 Push the hairpin into the lower part of the head under the chin to a depth of 13mm ($\frac{1}{2}$in), and place it onto the head base with the rounded end of the hairpin in the centre opening.

5 To make the arms, roll a thick finger rope of dough 7.5cm (3in) long. Cut the rope in half, and cut the ends straight with a knife. Make a hole 6mm ($\frac{1}{4}$in) from the tops of the arms with the drinking straw.

6 To make the legs, roll another thick finger rope 10cm (4in) long. Cut the rope in half, and cut the ends straight with a knife. Make a hole 6mm ($\frac{1}{4}$in) from the tops of the legs with the drinking straw.

7 Place the head, arms and legs onto a baking tray, and bake at 100°C (200°F or gas mark $\frac{1}{4}$) for about five hours.

8 When the dough has cooled, secure the hairpin in the head with a little fast-setting glue.

9 Make hanging loops for each piece by threading some sewing cotton through the loop of the hairpin and through the holes in the arms and legs and tying it off.

10 When the baked dough is cool, paint the head, arms and legs light grey. When the grey is dry, use pink paint for the ears and to paint the nails on the edges of the arms and legs.

11 Apply two coats of varnish.

12 To make the soft body, and to attach the head, arms and legs, see Techniques pages 10–11.

MAKING THE ELEPHANT'S CLOTHES

JACKET

1 Using tracing paper, make a copy of pattern no. 7 (see page 139).

2 Pin the pattern to a double layer of fabric and cut out. With right sides facing, stitch the two pieces together along the shoulder, side and underarm seams with a 6mm (¼in) seam allowance.

3 Fold the bodice in half, side seams together and crease. Unfold again and carefully cut straight up the foldline at the centre of the front of the jacket from the waist to the neckline.

4 Turn the jacket the right way out and put on the elephant. Sew two small beads or buttons to the front of the jacket to finish.

TROUSERS

1 Using tracing paper, make a copy of pattern no. 8 (see page 139).

2 Pin pattern to a double layer of fabric and cut out. With right sides together, and with a seam allowance of 6mm (¼in), sew the two pieces together – up both sides and along the inner leg seams.

3 Turn the trousers the right way out, put onto the elephant and secure with a couple of stitches to the body.

If you enjoyed making the mole or elephant, you could now try this **Teddy Bear** complete with baby teddy bear tucked in his coat pocket.

Actual size: height 15cm (6in)

MAKING THE HEAD, ARMS AND LEGS

1 Roll a ball of dough the size of a golf ball for the head. Roll a small ball for the nose and join it to the head. Smooth around the join with a damp paintbrush. Roll out another piece of dough thinly, cut a small triangle, and join it to the end of the nose. Make holes for the eyes with the point of a cocktail stick. Wet these holes and push a bead into each eye socket.

2 Make the ears from two small flattened balls of dough, and join them to the

Salt dough

75g (3oz) plain flour
40g (1$\frac{1}{2}$oz) table salt
40ml (1$\frac{1}{2}$fl oz or ³⁄₁₆ cup) water

In addition to your basic tools and equipment you will need:

Cocktail stick
2 small black beads for the eyes
1 hairpin cut to 25mm (1in)
Ready-made head base (see Techniques page 9)
Small sharp knife
Drinking straw (medium-hole)
Fast-setting glue
Black paint
30 x 11.5cm (12 x 4$\frac{1}{2}$in) felt fabric for the duffle coat
23 x 7.5cm (9 x 3in) fabric for the trousers

head. Push the hairpin into the lower part of the head under the chin to a depth of 13mm ($\frac{1}{2}$in), and position it in the head base with the rounded end of the hairpin in the centre opening.

3 To make the arms, roll a finger-sized rope of dough about 7.5cm (3in) long. Cut the rope in half and round off one end of each piece with your finger and thumb. Using a drinking straw, make a hole 6mm ($\frac{1}{4}$in) from the other end of the arm – at the shoulder.

4 To make the legs, roll another rope of dough 10cm (4in) long but slightly fatter than the arms. Cut it in half, round off one end of each piece, turning the feet slightly upwards. Make a hole 6mm ($\frac{1}{4}$in) from the tops of the legs with a drinking straw.

5 To make the pocket bear and the toggles for the duffle coat, see overleaf.

6 Place all the pieces onto a baking tray and bake at 100°C (200°F or gas mark $\frac{1}{4}$) for five hours.

7 When the dough has cooled, secure the hairpin in the head with a little fast-setting glue.

8 Thread some sewing cotton through the hole of the hairpin and the holes in the arms and legs and tie it off to make hanging loops for each piece.

TO MAKE THE TOGGLES FOR THE DUFFLE COAT

you will need:

Two cocktail sticks

Salt dough

1 Roll a tiny rope of dough 20mm ($\frac{3}{4}$in) long and cut it in half.

2 Push the point of a cocktail stick through the centre of each piece so that you make a hole right through. Leave the sticks in whilst baking to keep the holes open.

3 Bake the toggles with the dough character. When they are cool, remove the cocktail sticks, and then varnish.

AND TO MAKE THE POCKET TEDDY BEAR

you will need:

Cocktail stick

Salt dough

1 Roll a tiny, oval-shaped ball of dough for the body.

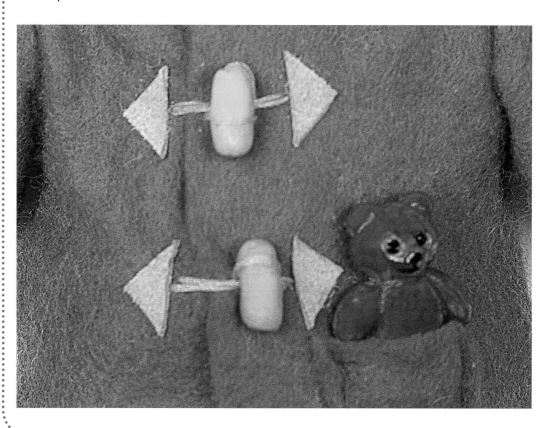

2 Roll a thin rope of dough, cut into four pieces for the arms and legs, and join these to the body.

3 Roll a tiny head, and two tiny ears, and attach them to the head. Make the eyes with a cocktail stick.

4 Lay the pocket bear on a baking tray and bake with the dough character.

5 When the dough is cool, paint the eyes and mouth black, and then varnish.

6 When the baked dough is cool, paint the teddy's nose and mouth black.

7 Apply two coats of varnish.

8 To make the soft body, and to attach the head, arms and legs, see Techniques pages 10–11.

MAKING THE TEDDY BEAR'S CLOTHES

DUFFLE COAT

1 Using tracing paper, make a copy of pattern no. 7 (see page 139).

2 Pin pattern to a double layer of fabric and cut out. With right sides facing, stitch the two pieces together along the shoulder, side and underarm seams with a 6mm ($\frac{1}{4}$in) seam allowance.

3 Fold the coat in half, side seams together and crease. Unfold again and carefully cut straight up the foldline at the centre of the front of the duffle coat from the waist to the neckline.

4 Turn the coat the right way out, put it onto the teddy bear. Stitch the toggles in position on the coat, wrapping the thread around them once and attaching through to the soft body. Cut four small triangles from a piece of fabric and glue in position opposite each other over where the thread goes through.

TROUSERS

1 Using tracing paper, make a copy of pattern no. 8 (see page 139).

2 Pin the pattern to a double layer of fabric and cut out. With right sides together, and with a seam allowance of 6mm ($\frac{1}{4}$in), sew the two pieces together – up both sides and along the inner leg seams.

3 Turn the trousers to the right side. Put them onto the teddy bear and secure with a couple of stitches to the body.

Harry Hedgehog

• • • • • • • • • • •

For the outdoors Harry
Hedgehog wears a fetching
knitted jumper, tartan trousers
and matching scarf. Why not
make a collection of the other
woodland characters to keep
him company?

Actual size: height 15cm (6in)

Salt dough

75g (3oz) plain flour
40g (1½oz) table salt
40ml (1½fl oz or ³⁄₁₆ cup) water

In addition to your basic tools and equipment you will need:

Garlic press
Cocktail stick
1 hairpin cut to 25mm (1in)
Ready-made head base (see Techniques page 9)
Small sharp knife
Drinking straw (medium-hole)
Fast-setting glue
Paints: black, brown and red
1 x 25g ball knitting wool (4-ply)
Pair of no. 3mm knitting needles to make the sweater
23 x 10cm (9 x 4in) fabric to make the trousers and scarf

TO MAKE THE HEAD, ARMS AND LEGS

1 Roll a ball of dough the size of a golf ball. Pinch out a small part for the nose and turn it slightly upwards. Roll two pea-sized balls of dough for the cheeks, and fix them either side of the nose. Smooth around the join with a damp paintbrush.

2 Push some dough through a garlic press to make hair.

3 Join the hair to the head, starting at the nose, and working your way around until the whole head is covered with strands of dough (*see photo opposite*).

4 Make holes for the eyes with the cocktail stick.

5 Roll a tiny ball of dough for the nose, and join it to the head.

6 Make two tiny ears from two small, flattened balls of dough and join them to the head.

7 Push the hairpin into the lower part of the head under the chin to a depth of 13mm (½in). Place on the head base.

Step 3 (page 48) Joining hair to the hedgehog's head

8 To make the arms, roll a finger-sized rope of dough 7.5cm (3in) long. Cut the rope in half and round off one end of each piece with your finger and thumb. At the shoulder end, make a hole 6mm ($^{1}/_{4}$in) from the top, with a drinking straw.

9 To make the legs, roll another rope of dough 10cm (4in) long. Cut it in half and round off one end of each piece. To create the hip joint, make a hole with a drinking straw 6mm ($^{1}/_{4}$in) from the other end.

10 Place all the pieces on a baking tray and bake at 100°C (200°F or gas mark $^{1}/_{4}$) for about five hours.

11 When the dough has cooled, secure the hairpin in the head with a little fast-setting glue. Make hanging loops for each piece by threading some sewing cotton through the loop of the hairpin and through the holes in the arms and legs and tying it off.

12 When the baked dough is cool, paint the hair brown, the nose black and the cheeks a watery red.

13 Apply two coats of varnish to all the dough parts.

14 To make the soft body, and to attach the head, arms and legs, see Techniques pages 10–11.

MAKING THE HEDGEHOG'S CLOTHES

KNITTING THE SWEATER – FRONT AND BACK ALIKE

1 For the front: cast on 22 stitches and work 3 rows in knit 1 – purl 1 rib.

2 Work in stocking stitch until work measures 5.5cm (2¼in). Cast off.

3 Repeat steps 1 and 2 to make the back of the sweater.

SLEEVES – BOTH ALIKE

1 For each sleeve: cast on 16 stitches and work 3 rows in knit 1 – purl 1 rib.

2 Work in stocking stitch until work measures 45mm (1¾in). Cast off.

TO ASSEMBLE THE SWEATER

1 With a 6mm (¼in) seam allowance, and right sides facing, sew the front to the back along one shoulder seam.

2 Sew in the sleeves, and then sew up the sides.

3 Turn the sweater the right way out, put it on the hedgehog and then stitch up the remaining shoulder seam.

TROUSERS

1 Using tracing paper, make a copy of pattern no. 8 (see page 139).

2 Pin the pattern to a double layer of fabric and cut out. With right sides together, and with a seam allowance of 6mm (¼in), sew the two pieces together – up both sides and along the inner leg seams.

3 Turn the trousers the right way out, put onto the elephant and secure with a couple of stitches to the body.

SCARF

1 Cut the fabric to measure 20 x 2.5cm (8 x 1in).

2 Tie around the hedgehog's neck.

Crazy Clown

• • • • • • • • • • •

This crazy clown character is colourful and flexible. He would make a fun addition to any toy box or bedroom shelf and provide hours of entertainment.

Actual size: height 15cm (6in)

Salt dough

75g (3oz) plain flour

40g (1$\frac{1}{2}$oz) table salt

40ml (1$\frac{1}{2}$fl oz or $\frac{3}{16}$ cup) water

In addition to your basic tools and equipment you will need:

Cocktail stick

2 small black beads for the eyes

Garlic press

1 hairpin cut to 25mm (1in)

Small sharp knife

Fast-setting glue

Drinking straw (medium-hole)

Paints: red and black

30 x 16.5cm (12 x 6$\frac{1}{2}$in) fabric for the top part of the suit and hat

23 x 10cm (9 x 4in) fabric for the trousers

3 or 4 small pom-poms for the front of the suit and hat

12.5cm (5in) ribbon for the neck

91.5cm (1yd) narrow ribbon for the cuffs and ankles

TO MAKE THE HEAD, ARMS AND LEGS

1 Roll a ball of dough the size of a table tennis ball for the head. Roll a tiny ball for the nose and join it to the head. Make holes for the eyes with a cocktail stick. Wet the holes and push a bead firmly into each eye socket.

2 Push some dough through a garlic press to make some hair. Cut the strands fairly short and join them to the head (*see photo overleaf*).

3 Push the hairpin into the lower part of the head under the chin to a depth of 13mm ($\frac{1}{2}$in).

4 To make the arms, roll a finger-sized rope of dough 7.5cm (3in) long. Cut the rope in half and round off one end of each piece with your finger and thumb. Cut a notch at one end of each arm for the thumbs. Make a hole 6mm ($\frac{1}{4}$in) in from the tops of the arms with the straw.

Step 2 (page 53) Joining the clown's hair to his head

5 To make the legs and shoes: roll another rope of dough 7.5cm (3in) long and cut it in half. Roll two marble-sized balls of dough for the shoes. Make a hole in the centre of each ball with your finger, and join them to the legs.

6 Roll two small balls of dough for pom-poms and join them to the front of the shoes. Make a hole 6mm ($\frac{1}{4}$in) in from the tops of the legs with a drinking straw.

7 Place all the pieces onto a baking tray and bake at 100°C (200°F or gas mark $\frac{1}{4}$) for about five hours.

8 When the dough has cooled, secure the hairpin in the head with a little fast-setting glue. Make hanging loops for each piece by threading some sewing cotton through the loop of the hairpin and through the holes in the arms and legs and tying it off.

9 When the baked dough is cool, paint the mouth black, and the nose and cheeks a watery red.

10 Apply two coats of varnish to all the dough parts.

11 To make the soft body, and to attach the head, arms and legs, see Techniques pages 10–11.

MAKING THE CLOWN'S CLOTHES

TOP

1 Using tracing paper, make a copy of pattern no. 7 (see page 139).

2 Pin the pattern to a double layer of fabric and cut out. With right sides facing, stitch the two pieces together along the shoulder, side and underarm seams with a 6mm ($\frac{1}{4}$in) seam allowance.

3 Fold the top in half, side seams together and crease. Unfold again and carefully cut 2.5cm (1in) down the centre foldline from the neckline to make the opening big enough for the head.

4 Put the top on the clown and slip stitch the back opening closed.

5 Run a gathering stitch around the cuffs and adjust the gathers to fit. Tie some narrow ribbon around the wrists.

6 Run a gathering stitch along the edge of the ribbon. Gather the ribbon to fit around the neck and stitch in place.

7 Sew some pom-poms to the front of the top.

TROUSERS

1 Using tracing paper, make a copy of pattern no. 8 (see page 139).

2 Pin pattern to a double layer of fabric and cut out. With right sides together, and with a seam allowance of 6mm ($\frac{1}{4}$in), sew the two pieces together – up both sides and along the inner leg seams.

3 Turn the trousers the right way out. Run a gathering stitch around the ankles, and adjust the gathers to fit. Tie some narrow ribbon around the ankles.

4 Put the trousers on the clown, and slip stitch to the waist of the body around the top.

HAT

1 Using tracing paper, make a copy of pattern no. 11 (see page 134).

2 Cut out of a double layer of fabric and, with a 6mm ($\frac{1}{4}$in) seam allowance, stitch along the seam.

3 Glue the hat to the clown's head, fold over the end and secure it with a few stitches.

4 Sew a pom-pom at the end to finish.

Footballer

• • • • • • • • • • • •

Little boys will love playing with this footballer. You could make a whole team sporting their favourite team strip!

Actual size: height 15cm (6in)

Salt dough

75g (3oz) plain flour

40g (1$\frac{1}{2}$oz) table salt

40ml (1$\frac{1}{2}$fl oz or $\frac{3}{16}$ cup) water

In addition to your basic tools and equipment you will need:

Cocktail stick

Garlic press

1 hairpin cut to 25mm (1in)

Ready-made head base (see Techniques page 9)

Small sharp knife

Drinking straw

Fast-setting glue

Paints: black, brown, white and blue

30 x 11.5cm (12 x 4$\frac{1}{2}$in) fabric for the shirt

23 x 7.5cm (9 x 3in) fabric for the shorts

TO MAKE THE HEAD, ARMS AND LEGS

1 Roll a ball of dough the size of a table tennis ball for the head. Roll a tiny ball for the nose and join it to the head.

2 Make holes for the eyes and mouth with a cocktail stick.

3 Push some dough through a garlic press to make some hair, and join it to the head.

4 Push the hairpin into the lower part of the head under the chin to a depth of 13mm ($\frac{1}{2}$in), and place the head onto the ready-made head base with the rounded end of the hairpin in the centre opening.

5 To make the arms, roll a finger-sized rope of dough 7.5cm (3in) long. Cut the rope in half and round off one end of each piece with your finger and thumb. Cut a notch at one end of each arm for the thumbs. Make a hole 6mm ($\frac{1}{4}$in) in from the tops of the arms with the drinking straw.

6 To make the legs and boots: roll another rope of dough 10cm (4in) long. Cut it in half, and round off one end of each piece. Turn up these ends for the football boots.

7 Roll a thin rope of dough, and join some around the ankles to form the tops of the boots. Roll out some dough

Step 7 (page 58) Making studs for the footballer's boots

thinly and cut two small pieces to fit around the centre of the legs to represent socks. Roll some tiny balls of dough for the studs on the boots, and join them (*see photo*).

8 Make a hole 6mm ($^1/_4$in) from the top of the legs with the drinking straw.

9 Place all the pieces onto a baking tray and bake at 120°C (240°F or gas mark $^1/_2$) for about four hours.

10 When the dough has cooled, secure the hairpin in the head with a little fast-setting glue. Make hanging loops for each piece by threading some sewing cotton through the loop of the hairpin and through the holes in the arms and legs and tying it off.

FINISHING THE HEAD, ARMS AND LEGS

11 When the baked dough is cool, paint the hair brown, and the eyes blue. Use black and white paint for the boots and socks.

12 Apply two coats of varnish to all the dough parts.

13 To make the soft body, and to attach the head, arms and legs, see Techniques pages 10–11.

CLOTHES FOR THE FOOTBALLER

SHIRT

1 Using tracing paper, make a copy of pattern no. 7 (see page 139).

2 Pin the pattern to a double layer of fabric and cut out. With right sides facing, stitch the two pieces together along the shoulder, side and underarm seams with a 6mm ($\frac{1}{4}$in) seam allowance.

3 Fold the top in half, side seams together and crease. Unfold again and, taking the front panel, carefully cut 4cm ($1\frac{1}{2}$in) down the centre foldline from the neckline.

4 Dress the footballer in his shirt.

SHORTS

1 Using tracing paper, make a copy of pattern no. 8 (see page 139).

2 Pin the pattern to a double layer of fabric and cut out. With right sides together, and with a seam allowance of 6mm ($\frac{1}{4}$in), sew the two pieces together – up both sides and along the inner leg seams.

3 Turn the shorts the right way out, put onto the footballer and secure with a couple of stitches to the body.

MAKING THE FOOTBALL

Roll a ball of dough in your hand the size of a large marble. Bake it with the other pieces and then paint it black and white.

Heavenly Angel

• • • • • • • • • •

You could hang this beautiful
angel in a window. It also makes
a perfect Christmas decoration.

Actual size: height 15cm (6in)

Salt dough

75g (3oz) plain flour
40g (1½oz) table salt
40ml (1½fl oz or ³⁄₁₆ cup) water

In addition to your basic tools and equipment you will need:

10cm (4in) gold wire for the halo
1 hairpin cut to 25mm (1in)
Ready-made head base (see Techniques page 9)
Small sharp knife
Drinking straw (medium-hole)
Fast-setting glue
Paints: black, gold and red
35.5 x 15cm (14 x 6in) white satin fabric for the robe
91.5cm (1yd) narrow gold braid
46cm (18in) thick gold thread

MAKING THE ANGEL'S HEAD, ARMS AND LEGS

1 Roll a ball of dough the size of a table tennis ball for the head. Roll a tiny ball for the nose and fix it to the head.

2 Roll a tiny rope shape in the palm of your hand, and curl it between your finger and thumb to make a hair curl. Make about another 40 of these curls, and join them to the head.

3 Bend the gold wire into a ring for the halo, finishing one end by continuing to twist it around the shaped wire. Leave the other end unsecured and then push it

into the head towards the back to fix the halo above the angel's head (*see photo overleaf*).

4 Push the hairpin into the lower part of the head under the chin to a depth of 13mm (½in) and place it onto the head base with the rounded end of the hairpin sitting in the centre opening.

5 To make the arms, roll a finger-sized rope of dough 7.5cm (3in) long. Cut the rope in half, and round off one end of each piece with your finger and thumb. Cut

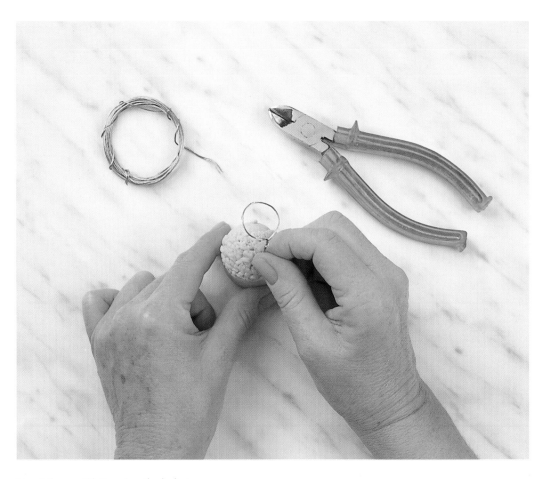

Step 3 (page 63) Securing the halo to the angel's head

a thumb and make some indentations for the fingers using the knife. Make a hole 6mm (¹⁄₄in) from the top of the arms with a drinking straw.

6 To make the legs, roll another rope of dough 10cm (4in) long. Cut it in half, round off one end of each piece and turn up the rounded ends for the feet.

7 Make some indentations for the toes with a knife. To create the hip joint, make a hole with a drinking straw 6mm (¹⁄₄in) from the other end.

8 See opposite for instructions on how to make the wings.

9 Place all the pieces on a baking tray and bake at 120°C (240°F or gas mark ¹⁄₂) for about three hours.

10 When the dough has cooled, secure the hairpin in the head with a little fast-setting glue. Make hanging loops for each piece to make them easier to paint and varnish: thread some sewing cotton through the loop of the hairpin and through the holes in the arms and legs and tie it off.

11 When the baked dough is cool, paint the eyes black, and mix together red and white to make pink for the cheeks and lips. Use gold for the hair and brush a little gold on the feet too.

12 Apply two coats of varnish to all parts.

13 To make the soft body, and to attach the head, arms and legs, see Techniques pages 10–11.

MAKING THE ANGEL'S DRESS

1 Using tracing paper, make a copy of pattern no. 1 (see page 141).

2 Pin the pattern to a double layer of fabric and cut out. Stitch the two pieces together along the shoulder, side and underarm seams with a 6mm ($1/4$in) seam allowance.

3 Fold the dress in half, side seams together and crease. Unfold again and carefully cut straight up the foldline at the centre of the back of the dress from the waist to the neckline; this will form the centre-back seam of the dress.

4 Turn up a 13mm ($1/2$in) hem at the bottom of the dress and around the sleeves. Stitch.

5 Stitch the gold trim to the skirt and sleeves of dress.

6 Put the dress on the angel and slip stitch closed the opening at the back.

7 Wind the gold thread around, creating a criss-cross at the front of the dress, and tying it tight at the back.

8 With several firm stitches, secure the wings at the back of the dress.

TO MAKE THE WINGS FOR THE ANGEL

you will need:

Salt Dough
Drinking straw (medium-hole)
Paints: blue, white and gold

1 Make a copy of the template (see page 140).

2 Roll out the dough 6mm ($1/4$in) thick and cut out the wings. Make two holes in the centre with a drinking straw. Bake the wings with the dough character.

3 When the dough is cool, use pale blue and white paints to create an effect of sky and cotton-wool clouds and then use gold to paint a border all around the wings. Apply two coats of varnish, and then stitch them firmly to the back of the dress.

Mountain Mouse

• • • • • • • • • • •

This mouse is wrapped up against the cold in a knitted outfit complete with woolly hat. He makes a good companion for the other woodland characters such as Harry Hedgehog and Digger Mole.

Actual size: height 15cm (6in)

Salt dough

50g (2oz) plain flour

25g (1oz) table salt

25ml (1fl oz or $\frac{1}{8}$ cup) water

In addition to your basic tools and equipment you will need:

Cocktail stick

3 small black beads for the eyes and nose

2 black stamens for the whiskers (available from craft shops)

Small sharp knife

1 hairpin cut to 25mm (1in)

Drinking straw (medium-hole)

Fast-setting glue

Paints: brown, pink and black

1 x 50g ball knitting wool (4-ply) for the sweater, trousers and hat

Pair of no. 3mm knitting needles

TO MAKE THE HEAD, ARMS AND LEGS

1 Roll a ball of dough the size of a golf ball, and pinch out one piece for the nose. Make a hole at the end of the nose with a cocktail stick. Wet the hole and push in a black bead.

2 Use the cocktail stick to make holes for the eyes, wet the holes, and push a bead into each eye socket.

3 Make the ears from two small, flattened balls of dough; curl them slightly, and fix them to the head.

4 Cut the stamens into six equal lengths. Push the ends into either side of the nose to act as whiskers (*see photo opposite*).

5 Push the hairpin into the lower part of the head under the chin to a depth of 13mm ($\frac{1}{2}$in).

6 To make the arms, roll a finger-sized rope of dough about 7.5cm (3in) long. Cut the rope in half and round off one end of each arm with your finger and thumb. Using a drinking straw, make a hole 6mm ($\frac{1}{4}$in) from the other end of the arm – at the shoulder.

7 To make the legs, roll another rope 10cm (4in) long. Cut it in half and round off one end of each piece with your finger and thumb. Turn up the rounded ends for the boots. Roll a thin rope and join

Step 4 (page 68) Inserting the mouse's whiskers

a piece around the ankles to complete the boots. Make a hole 6mm ($\frac{1}{4}$in) from the tops of the legs with a drinking straw.

8 Place the head, arms and legs onto a baking tray and bake at 100°C (200°F or gas mark $\frac{1}{4}$) for about five hours.

9 When the dough has cooled put some fast-setting glue around the holes of the hairpin, to keep it in place.

10 Thread some sewing cotton through the hole of the hairpin and holes in the arms and legs and tie it off to make hanging loops for each piece.

11 When the baked dough is cool, paint the head, arms and legs brown; the insides of the ears pink; and the boots black.

12 Apply two coats of varnish.

13 To make the soft body, and to attach the head, arms and legs, see Techniques pages 10–11.

MAKING THE MOUSE'S CLOTHES

KNITTING THE SWEATER – FRONT AND BACK ALIKE

1 For the front: cast on 22 stitches and work 3 rows in knit 1 – purl 1 rib.

2 Work in stocking stitch until work measures 5.5cm ($2\frac{1}{4}$in). Cast off.

3 Repeat steps 1 and 2 to make the back of the sweater.

SLEEVES – BOTH ALIKE

1 For each sleeve: cast on 16 stitches and work 3 rows in knit 1 – purl 1 rib.

2 Work in stocking stitch for 16 rows, or until work measures 4.5cm (1 3/4in). Cast off.

KNITTING THE TROUSERS – FRONT AND BACK ALIKE

1 For the front: cast on 22 stitches and work 3 rows in knit 1 – purl 1 rib.

2 Work in stocking stitch until work measures 4cm (1 1/2in).

3 Slip the next 11 stitches onto a spare needle and continue to work the remaining 11 stitches until work measures 5cm (2in). Work 3 rows in knit 1 – purl 1 rib and then cast off.

4 Rejoin wool to the remaining 11 stitches and work in stocking stitch until work measures 5cm (2in) from the beginning. Work 3 rows in knit 1 – purl 1 rib and then cast off.

5 Repeat steps 1 – 4 to make the other half of the trousers.

HAT

1 Cast on 30 stitches and work 6 rows in stocking stitch, ending on a purl row.

2 Next row: knit 10 stitches, yarn round needle and knit 2 stitches together; knit 6 stitches, yarn around needle and knit 2 stitches together. Knit to the end.

3 Work a further 13 rows in stocking stitch and then cast off.

TO MAKE UP THE KNITTED SUIT AND HAT FOR MOUSE

SWEATER

1 With a 6mm (1/4in) seam allowance, and right sides facing, sew the front to the back along one shoulder seam.

2 Sew in the sleeves, and then stitch the side seams.

3 Turn the right way out, put the sweater on the mouse, and slip stitch closed the remaining shoulder seam.

TROUSERS

1 With a 6mm (1/4in) seam allowance, and right sides facing, sew the two pieces together at the sides and inner legs.

2 Turn the trousers the right way out, put on the mouse, and slip stitch in place at the top.

HAT

1 Stitch the side seam. With a length of wool threaded onto a needle, run a gathering stitch across the top and tighten it to close the top of the hat. Secure with a few firm stitches and cast off.

Alternatively

If you enjoyed making the mouse, why not try this **Porky Pig** who wears the same knitted woolly outfit.

Actual size: height 15cm (6in)

MAKING THE HEAD, ARMS AND LEGS

1 Roll a ball of dough the size of a golf ball for the head. Roll a small rope about the thickness of a finger, cut from it a piece 13mm (¹/₂in) long, and join that to the head for the snout.

2 Make holes in the snout with a cocktail stick. Then make the mouth. Roll a tiny ball of dough and flatten it; cut it in half; curl it with your finger and thumb; and then fix it under the snout.

Salt dough

50g (2oz) plain flour

25g (1oz) table salt

25ml (1fl oz or $\frac{1}{8}$ cup) water

In addition to your basic tools and equipment you will need:

Cocktail stick

2 small black beads for the eyes

1 hairpin cut to 25mm (1in)

Ready-made head base (see Techniques page 9)

Small sharp knife

Drinking straw (medium-hole)

Fast-setting glue

1 x 50g ball knitting wool (4-ply) for the sweater and trousers

Pair no. 3mm knitting needles

3 Roll two pea-sized balls of dough for the cheeks, and join them either side of the snout. Smooth around the edges of the cheeks with a damp paintbrush.

4 Take two tiny balls of dough for the ears, roll them into ropes and then squeeze them into pig's ear shapes. Join these quite high on the back of the head.

5 Make holes for the eyes with a cocktail stick, wet the holes and push a bead into each eye socket.

6 Push the hairpin into the lower part of the head under the chin to a depth of 13mm ($\frac{1}{2}$in) and place it onto the head base, with the rounded end of the hairpin sitting in the centre opening.

7 To make the arms, roll a finger-sized rope of dough about 7.5cm (3in) long. Cut the rope in half and cut a notch at one end of each arm for the trotters. At the shoulder end, make a hole 6mm ($\frac{1}{4}$in) from the top, with a drinking straw.

8 To make the legs, roll another rope of dough 10cm (4in) long. Cut it in half and cut a notch at the ends of the legs. Make a hole with a drinking straw 6mm ($\frac{1}{4}$in) from the other end.

9 Place all the pieces on a baking tray and bake at 100°C (200°F or gas mark $\frac{1}{4}$) for about five hours.

10 When the dough has cooled, secure the hairpin in the head with a little

fast-setting glue. Make hanging loops for each piece by threading some sewing cotton through the loop of the hairpin and through the holes in the arms and legs and tying it off.

11 When the baked dough is cool, paint the cheeks pink and then apply two coats of varnish.

12 To make the soft body, and to attach the head, arms and legs, see Techniques pages 10–11.

KNITTING THE PIG'S CLOTHES

SWEATER – FRONT AND BACK ALIKE
1 For the front: cast on 22 stitches and work 3 rows in knit 1 – purl 1 rib.

2 Work in stocking stitch until work measures 5.5cm (2^1/$_4$in). Cast off.

3 Repeat steps 1 and 2 to make the back of the sweater.

SLEEVES – BOTH ALIKE
1 For each sleeve: cast on 16 stitches and work 3 rows in knit 1 – purl 1 rib.

2 Work 16 rows in stocking stitch, and then cast off.

TROUSERS – FRONT AND BACK ALIKE
1 For the front: cast on 22 stitches and work 3 rows in knit 1 – purl 1 rib.

2 Work in stocking stitch until work measures 4cm (1^1/$_2$in).

3 Slip the first 11 stitches onto a spare needle, and continue to work the remaining 11 stitches until work measures 5cm (2in). Work 3 rows in knit 1 – purl 1 rib and then cast off.

4 Rejoin wool to the remaining 11 stitches and work in stocking stitch until work measures 5cm (2in) from the beginning. Work 3 rows in knit 1 – purl 1 rib and then cast off.

5 Repeat steps 1– 4 to make the back half of the trousers.

TO MAKE UP THE PIG'S CLOTHES

SWEATER
1 With a 6mm (^{1}/$_4$in) seam allowance, and right sides facing, sew the front to the back along one shoulder seam.

2 Sew in the sleeves, and then stitch the side seams.

3 Turn the right way out, put the sweater on the pig, and slip stitch closed the remaining shoulder seam.

TROUSERS
1 With a 6mm (^{1}/$_4$in) seam allowance, and right sides facing, sew the two pieces together at the sides and inner legs.

2 Turn the right way out, put on the pig, and slip stitch in place at the top.

Teddy Bear Wedding

• • • • • • • • • • •

This teddy bear bride and groom

presented in a pretty basket

would make a wonderful and

personal wedding gift.

Actual size:
Basket height 24cm (10in)
Figures height 15cm (6in)

Salt dough

50g (2oz) plain flour

25g (1oz) table salt

25ml (1fl oz or $\frac{1}{8}$ cup) water

In addition to your basic tools and equipment you will need:

Small sharp knife

Cocktail stick

2 small black beads for the eyes

1 hairpin cut to 25mm (1in)

Drinking straw (medium-hole)

Fast-setting glue

Paints: black, white and red

66 x 10cm (26 x 4in) white fabric for the dress

15cm (6in) lace as decorative edging

20cm (8in) ribbon for around the waist

22.5 x 10cm (10 x 4in) fabric for the knickers

15 x 7.5cm (6 x 3in) white net or tulle for the veil

Teddy Bear Bride

TO MAKE THE HEAD, ARMS AND LEGS

1 Roll a ball of dough the size of a table tennis ball for the teddy's head. Roll a marble-sized ball for the snout, roll it between your finger and thumb, and join it to the head. Smooth around the join with a damp paintbrush.

2 Roll out another piece of dough thinly, cut a small triangle, and join it to the end of the nose.

3 Roll a small ball of dough for the ears. Cut it in half and flatten it on a work surface. Curl the ears slightly forward, and join them to the head.

4 Make holes for the eyes with a cocktail stick. Wet these holes and push a bead into each eye socket.

5 Roll up thin ropes of dough to make tiny individual roses and join them to the top of the head (*see photo opposite*).

Step 5 (page 76) Joining roses to the bride's head

6 Push the hairpin into the lower part of the head under the chin to a depth of 13mm (¹/₂in), and place it onto a baking tray.

7 To make the arms, roll a finger-sized rope of dough about 7.5cm (3in) long. Cut the rope in half and round off one end of each piece with your finger and thumb. Make three indentations in this end with the knife to represent the paws. Using a drinking straw, make a hole 6mm (¹/₄in) from the other end of the arm – at the shoulder.

8 To make the legs and shoes, roll another rope of dough 10cm (4in) long. Cut it in half, round off one end of each piece, turning the feet slightly upwards. Make a small ball of dough, flatten it and wrap it around the base of the foot to make the shoes. Make a hole 6mm (¹/₄in) from the tops of the legs with a drinking straw.

9 Prepare the bride's bouquet (see instructions on page 79).

10 Place all the pieces onto a baking tray with the head and bake at 100°C (200°F or gas mark ¹/₄) for about five hours.

11 When the dough has cooled, secure the hairpin in the head with a little fast-setting glue. Make hanging loops for each piece by threading some sewing cotton through the loop of the hairpin and through the holes in the arms and legs and tying it off.

11 Paint the nose black, the cheeks pink and also the roses. Then paint her shoes white and the buttons on them pink.

12 Apply two coats of varnish.

13 To make the teddy's soft body, and to attach the head, arms and legs, see Techniques pages 10–11.

MAKING THE TEDDY BEAR BRIDE'S CLOTHES

DRESS

1 Using tracing paper, make copies of pattern nos. 2 and 3 (see pages 135–136).

2 Pin pattern no. 2 to a double layer of fabric and cut out. Stitch the two pieces together along the shoulder, side and underarm seams with a 6mm (1/4in) seam allowance.

3 Fold the bodice in half, side seams together and crease. Unfold again and carefully cut straight up the foldline at the centre of the back of the bodice from the waist to the neckline; this will form the centre-back seam of the dress.

4 Using a double thickness of fabric, cut out pattern no. 3 for the skirt. Run a gathering stitch across the top and, with right sides together, join the top of the dress to the skirt at the waist.

5 Turn up a 6mm (1/4in) hem at the bottom of the dress. Stitch.

6 With right sides together, stitch the centre-back seam of the dress, leaving a 5cm (2in) opening at the top.

7 Put the dress on the bride, and slip stitch closed the opening at the back.

8 Stitch some lace around the sleeves with small running stitches, and pull the stitches to gather the sleeves around the arms.

9 Tie the ribbon in a bow at the back of the waist.

TO MAKE THE VEIL

1 Make a gathering stitch across the piece of tulle or net, gather the stitches tight and cast off.

2 Glue the veil to the bride's head.

KNICKERS

1 Using tracing paper, make a copy of pattern no. 5 (see page 138).

2 Cut it out twice in fabric, and with right sides together, stitch the side and inner leg seams, with a 6mm (1/4in) seam allowance.

3 Stitch some lace around the bottom of the fabric with small running stitches and tighten the stitches to fit the knickers around the legs.

FOR THE BRIDE'S BOUQUET

Step 2 Making the bride's bouquet

you will need:

Small amount of salt dough
Round cutter 25mm (1in) in diameter
Pink paint

1 Roll out some dough thinly and cut out a circle with the cutter.

2 Make six tiny roses (see instructions for making a rose on page 76 step 5) and join them to the centre of the circle (*see photo above*).

3 Take the circle of roses in your hand, and then wrap the circle around the roses to form a bouquet.

4 Bake the bouquet with the dough characters. When the dough has cooled, paint the roses pink, and apply two coats of varnish to the bouquet.

5 When you have dressed the bride, glue the bouquet to her hand. Then position her with the groom in the decorated wedding basket.

Teddy Bear Bridegroom

MAKING THE HEAD, ARMS AND LEGS

1 Roll a ball of dough the size of a golf ball for the teddy's head. Roll a marble-sized ball for the snout, roll it between your finger and thumb, and join it to the head. Smooth around the join with a damp paintbrush.

2 Roll out another piece of dough thinly, cut a small triangle, and join it to the end of the nose.

3 Roll a small ball of dough for the ears. Flatten it on a work surface and cut it in half. Curl the ears slightly forward, and join them to the head.

4 Make holes for the eyes with a cocktail stick. Wet these holes and push a bead into each eye socket.

5 Push the hairpin into the lower part of the head under the chin to a depth of 13mm ($^1/_2$in), and position it in the head base with the rounded end of the hairpin in the centre opening.

6 To make the arms, roll a finger-sized rope of dough about 7.5cm (3in) long. Cut the rope in half and round off one end of each piece. Make three indentations in this end with the knife to represent the paws. Using a drinking straw, make a hole 6mm ($^1/_4$in) from the other end of the arm – at the shoulder.

7 To make the legs and boots, roll two more finger-sized ropes of dough: one should be 10cm (4in) long and the other, for the boots, should be 5cm (2in) long. Cut both in half. Make a hole 6mm ($^1/_4$in) from the tops of the longer leg pieces with a drinking straw.

Salt dough

75g (3oz) plain flour

40g (1$^1/_2$oz) table salt

40ml (1$^1/_2$fl oz or $^3/_{16}$ cup) water

In addition to your basic tools and equipment you will need:

Small sharp knife

Cocktail stick

2 small black beads for the eyes

1 hairpin cut to 25mm (1in)

Ready-made head base (see Techniques page 9)

Drinking straw (medium-hole)

Fast-setting glue

Paints: black and gold

30 x 7.5cm (12 x 3in) fabric for the jacket

1 small bead or button for fastening the jacket

23 x 7.5cm (9 x 3in) fabric for the trousers

5cm (2in) narrow lace

Step 8 Making the bridegroom's boots

8 Take the shorter boot pieces and turn up one end of each piece. Put your finger into the centre of the top of the boots and press them gently onto a work surface (this will flatten the sole part and shape the boots). With a knife, cut a small opening down the front of the boots (*see photo above*).

9 Join the boots to the ends of the legs. Cut two small pieces of dough for the tongues of the boots and fix them in position. Trim off any excess dough at the top of the boots with a knife. Make holes for the laces with a cocktail stick.

10 Place all the pieces onto a baking tray with the head and bake at 100°C (200°F or gas mark $1/4$) for about five hours.

11 When the dough has cooled, secure the hairpin in the head with a little

fast-setting glue. Make hanging loops for each piece by threading some sewing cotton through the loop of the hairpin and through the holes in the arms and legs and tying it off.

12 When the baked dough is cool, paint the nose and mouth black, and the boots gold.

13 Apply two coats of varnish.

14 To make the soft body, and to attach the head, arms and legs, see Techniques pages 10–11.

MAKING THE BRIDEGROOM'S CLOTHES

JACKET

1 Using tracing paper, make a copy of pattern no. 7 (see page 139).

2 Pin the pattern to a double layer of fabric and cut out. With right sides facing, stitch the two pieces together along the shoulder, side and underarm seams with a 6mm (¼in) seam allowance.

3 Fold the jacket in half, side seams together, and crease. Unfold again and carefully cut straight up the foldline at the centre of the front of the jacket from the waist to the neckline. Cut a curve to the lower front corners of the jacket.

4 Gather the lace and sew it to the front of the body as the front of a dress shirt.

5 Put the jacket on the bridegroom, secure with a couple of stitches at the front and sew beads in position for buttons. Glue the buttonhole to the lapel (see below for instructions).

TROUSERS

1 Using tracing paper, make a copy of pattern no. 8 (see page 139).

2 Pin pattern to a double layer of fabric and cut out. With right sides together, and with a seam allowance of 6mm ($^1/_4$in), sew the two pieces together – up both sides and along the inner leg seams.

3 Turn the trousers the right way out, put onto the bridegroom and secure with a couple of stitches to the body.

FOR THE BRIDEGROOM'S BUTTONHOLE

you will need:

Tiny amount of salt dough

Fast-setting glue

Pink paint

1 Make a tiny rose (see instructions for making a rose on page 76 step 5).

2 Bake the rose with the dough characters. When the dough is cool, paint the rose pink, varnish it, and then glue it to the bridegroom's jacket.

TO MAKE THE BRIDEGROOM'S BOW TIE

you will need:

Felt or narrow ribbon

Fast-setting glue

1 Cut out a small bow tie shape from felt or ribbon and using a small amount of glue, stick it in place.

Decorating the Basket

TO LINE THE BASKET

you will need:

Fibre filling

Satin material

Lace

Needle and thread

1 Line the basket with fibre filling.

2 Cut out some satin material large enough to line the basket and tack it through the bottom and sides.

3 Edge and tack lace around the edge.

TO MAKE TWELVE ROSES TO DECORATE THE WEDDING BASKET

you will need:

Small amount of salt dough

Small leaf-shaped cutter

Two straight hairpins

Wire cutters

Florist's wire

1 With the wire cutters, cut the hairpins into 13mm ($\frac{1}{2}$in) lengths, each hairpin making about six short lengths. Pinch the ends together to form an eyelet hole.

Step 5 (page 84) Making the roses for the basket

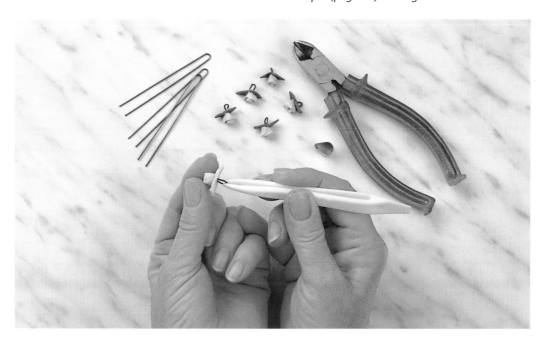

2 Roll out thinly a small amount of dough, and cut out twenty-four leaves with the leaf cutter. Join two leaves together at the rounded ends.

3 Roll a tiny rope of dough, flatten it and curl it into a bud.

4 Roll two tiny balls, flatten them into petals and join them around the bud.

5 Attach the rose to a pair of leaves, and push an eyelet into the bottom of the leaves at the centre so that it protrudes slightly (*see photo page 83*).

6 Make another eleven roses in the same way. Lay the roses on a baking tray, and bake at 120°C (250°F or gas mark $^1/_2$) for about two hours.

7 When the dough has cooled, paint the roses pink and varnish them.

TO ATTACH THE ROSES TO THE BASKET

1 Thread a length of florist's wire through the hole of a rose's eyelet, and twist the wire under the eyelet to keep the rose firmly in place.

2 Position the rose and secure it by winding the end of the florist's wire tightly around the handle of the basket (*see photo below*).

3 Add the remaining roses in the same way to cover the handle.

Step 2 Attaching the roses to the basket

Step 2 Making the wedding bells

TO MAKE WEDDING BELLS FOR THE BASKET

you will need:

Salt dough

Two cocktail sticks

Silver paint

Two small pearl beads

1 Roll a small ball of dough and shape it into the form of a bell.

2 Push a cocktail stick right through the bell from the bottom to extend out through to the top (*see photo above*). Leave this in place when the dough is baked to keep the hole open. Repeat steps 1 and 2 to make another bell.

3 Lay the bells on a baking tray, and bake at 120°C (250°F or gas mark $\frac{1}{2}$) for about two hours.

4 When the dough has cooled, remove the cocktail sticks. Paint the bells silver and apply two coats of varnish.

5 Thread a pearl bead onto some cotton and secure it.

6 Thread the needle through the hole in the bell and attach to the top of the wedding basket.

Step 2 Making the hearts for the basket

TO MAKE THE HEARTS FOR THE WEDDING BASKET

you will need:

Salt dough
Medium-sized heart-shaped cutter
Drinking straw (small-hole)
Paint: pink, blue and white
2 pearl beads

1 Roll out some dough thinly and cut out two hearts.

2 Roll a long, very thin rope of dough, and use this to write the names of the bride and groom. Attach the names to the hearts (*see photo above*).

3 Make a hole at the top of the hearts with the drinking straw.

4 Place on a baking tray with the bells and the roses and bake them at 120°C (250°F or gas mark ½) for about two hours.

5 When the dough has cooled, paint the bride's name in pink and the groom's in blue. Varnish, and then sew them to the handle of the basket; a pearl bead threaded onto the cotton will add the special finishing touch.

Frog
Fisherman

● ● ● ● ● ● ● ● ● ●

With his fishing rod and waders,
Frog Fisherman is ready for the
fish to bite. He would make a
good companion for the other
woodland characters such as
Digger Mole and Harry
Hedgehog.

Actual size: height 17.5cm (7in)

Salt dough

75g (3oz) plain flour

40g (1½oz) table salt

40ml (1½fl oz or $^3/_{16}$ cup) water

In addition to your basic tools and equipment you will need:

Small sharp knife

2 small black beads for the eyes

3 cocktail sticks

1 hairpin cut to 25mm (1in)

Ready-made head base (see Techniques page 9)

Drinking straw (medium-hole)

Fast-setting glue

Paints: green and red

30 x 11.5cm (12 x 4½in) waterproof fabric for the coat

2 small buttons or beads

23 x 7.5cm (9 x 3in) fabric for the trousers

Small amount of double-knitting wool for the scarf

Pair no. 3mm knitting needles

7.5 x 4cm (3 x 1½in) fabric for the hat

TO MAKE THE HEAD, ARMS AND LEGS

1 Roll a ball of dough the size of a golf ball for the head. Pinch out a piece for the mouth, and divide the upper and lower jaw with a knife.

2 Roll two pea-sized balls of dough for the eyes and fix them on the top of the head. Push a bead into each eyehole.

3 Roll a tiny ball for the nose and join it to the top of the mouth. With a cocktail stick, make two holes in the nose.

4 Push the hairpin into the lower part of the head under the chin to a depth of 13mm (½in), and position it in the head base with the rounded end of the hairpin in the centre opening.

Step 9 Attaching the frog's legs to the waders

5 To make the arms, roll a finger-sized rope of dough about 9cm (3½in) long. Cut the rope in half and cut some fingers with a knife.

6 Push a cocktail stick into one of the hands as a fishing rod; leave it in place when you bake the dough. Using a drinking straw, make a hole 6mm (¼in) from the other end of each arm – at the shoulder.

7 To make the legs and waders, roll another rope of dough 10cm (4in) long. Cut it in half and turn up one end of each leg with your finger and thumb. Holding one wader between your finger and thumb, press a finger from your other hand into the middle of the top, and then pull up the outer edges, bringing the sides

slightly higher than the fronts, to form the waders. Put them aside while you make the top part of the leg.

8 Roll a third small rope of dough, this time 5cm (2in) long. Cut it in half and, with the drinking straw, make a hole 13mm (½in) from the top of each leg.

9 Break off the points of 2 cocktail sticks, and push them into the tops of the waders, leaving about 13mm (½in) sticking out. Push the tops of the legs onto the ends of the sticks, to join the legs and waders, making sure that there is a space between the bottom of the legs and the top inside of the waders (*see photo above*).

10 Place all the pieces onto a baking tray and bake at 100°C (200°F or gas mark $1/4$) for about five hours.

11 When the dough has cooled, secure the hairpin in the head with a little fast-setting glue.

12 Thread some cotton through the hole of the hairpin and the holes in the arms and legs and tie it off to make hanging loops for each piece – to make them easier to paint and varnish.

13 When the baked dough is cool, paint the frog's head, arms and waders green, and the mouth red.

14 Apply two coats of varnish.

15 To make the soft body, and to attach the head, arms and legs, see Techniques pages 10–11.

MAKING THE FROG FISHERMAN'S CLOTHES

COAT

1 Using tracing paper, make a copy of pattern no. 7 (see page 139).

2 Pin the pattern to a double layer of fabric and cut out. With right sides facing, stitch the two pieces together along the shoulder, side and underarm seams with a 6mm ($1/4$in) seam allowance.

3 Fold the coat in half, side seams together and crease. Unfold again and carefully cut straight up the foldline at the centre of the front of the coat from the waist to the neckline.

4 Turn the coat the right way out and put it on the frog, securing it at the front with two buttons or beads.

TROUSERS

1 Using tracing paper, make a copy of pattern no. 8 (see page 139).

2 Pin the pattern to a double layer of fabric and cut out. With right sides together, and with a 6mm ($1/4$in) seam allowance, stitch together the front and back pieces along the side and inner leg seams.

3 Turn the trousers the right way out, put them on the frog, and glue the ends of the trouser legs to the inside of the waders (*see photo overleaf*).

4 Slip stitch the top of the trousers to the body around the waist.

SCARF

1 Cast on 22 stitches and work 12 rows in knit 1 – purl 1 rib. Cast off.

2 Wrap the scarf around the frog's neck and slip stitch together the edges to form a seam at the back.

Step 3 (page 91) Gluing the frog's trousers into his waders

HAT

1 Using tracing paper, make a copy of pattern no. 10 (see page 134).

2 Cut out the shape from a double thickness of fabric. With right sides together, and with a 6mm ($^1/_4$in) seam allowance, stitch the back seams together.

3 Turn the hat the right way out, place it on the frog's head and secure it by stitching it to the back of the scarf.

FINISHING

A tiny piece of kitchen foil threaded onto a length of cotton makes the ideal fish and fishing line for the fishing rod.

Intrepid Explorer

. . . .

Complete with handy backpack
and sturdy walking boots, this
intrepid explorer is ready for
any kind of adventure.

Actual size: height 17.5cm (7in)

Salt dough

100g (4oz) plain flour

50g (2oz) table salt

50ml (2fl oz or $\frac{1}{4}$ cup) water

In addition to your basic tools and equipment you will need:

3 cocktail sticks

Garlic press

1 hairpin cut to 25mm (1in)

Ready-made head base (see Techniques page 9)

Small sharp knife

Drinking straw (medium-hole)

Fast-setting glue

Paints: cream, blue, brown, red, green, black and white

1 x 25g ball knitting wool (4-ply) for the sweater

Pair of no. 3mm knitting needles

23 x 7.5cm (9 x 3in) fabric for the trousers

20.5 x 7.5cm (8 x 7.5in) fabric for the waistcoat

15.5 x 5cm (6 x 2in) fabric to make the backpack

35.5cm (14in) bias binding to trim the backpack

TO MAKE THE HEAD, ARMS, LEGS AND BOOTS

1 Roll a ball of dough the size of a table tennis ball for the head. Roll a tiny ball for the nose, and join it to the head. Make a hole for the mouth with the cocktail stick.

2 Roll a small ball of dough for the hat and press your finger into the centre to make the main part of the hat. Roll out some dough thinly and cut a peak shape from it. Fix the hat on the head, and join the peak to the hat.

3 Push some dough through a garlic press to make hair and join some strands of dough around the head.

4 Push the hairpin into the lower part of the head under the chin to a depth of 13mm ($\frac{1}{2}$in), and place the head onto the head base with the rounded end of the hairpin in the centre opening.

Step 7 Making the explorer's boots

5 To make the arms, roll a small rope of dough about 9cm (3$\frac{1}{2}$in) long. Cut the rope in half and round off one end of each arm with your finger and thumb. Press the rounded ends slightly to form the hands, and cut a thumb with a knife. Using a drinking straw, make a hole 6mm ($\frac{1}{4}$in) from the other end of the arm.

6 Roll another rope of dough 10cm (4in) long for the legs. Cut it in half and then cover the pieces with a damp teacloth to stop them drying out while you make the explorer's boots.

7 For each boot, roll a small rope of dough 4cm (1$\frac{1}{2}$in) long. Turn up one end to form the toe of the boot. Make a hole in the top of the boot with a knife and work your way around the inside edge with the point of the knife, carefully lifting out

the dough from inside to create hollow boots (*see photo above*). Roll a very thin rope of dough for the laces and join them to the front of the boot.

8 Take the two pieces of dough from under the teacloth. Break or cut off the points of 2 cocktail sticks, and push them into the tops of the legs, leaving about 6mm ($\frac{1}{4}$in) sticking out. Cut two strips of dough for the socks, and join them to the legs. Make some indentations on the socks with the knife.

9 Wet the inside of the top of the boots and push the ends of the cocktail sticks into the boots to join the legs and boots. With the drinking straw, make a hole 6mm ($\frac{1}{4}$in) from the top of each leg.

10 Place the head on its head base, together with the arms and booted legs, onto a baking tray, and bake at 120°C (240°F or gas mark $^1/_2$) for about four hours.

11 When the dough has cooled put some fast-setting glue around the holes of the hairpin, to keep it in place.

12 Thread some sewing cotton through the hole of the hairpin and the holes in the arms and legs and tie it off to make hanging loops for each piece – to make them easier to paint and varnish.

12 When the baked dough is cool, paint the hat green and the socks cream. Use brown for the hair, eyebrows and boots, watery red for the cheeks and the inside of the mouth and white, blue and black for the eyes. Apply two coats of varnish to all the pieces.

13 To make the soft body, and to attach the head, arms and legs, see Techniques pages 10–11.

MAKING THE EXPLORER'S CLOTHES AND BACKPACK

KNITTING THE SWEATER – FRONT AND BACK ALIKE

1 For the front: cast on 22 stitches and work 3 rows in knit 1 – purl 1 rib.

2 Work in stocking stitch until work measures 5.5cm (2$^1/_4$in). Cast off.

3 Repeat steps 1 and 2 to make the back of the sweater.

SLEEVES – BOTH ALIKE

1 For each sleeve: cast on 16 stitches and work 3 rows in knit 1 – purl 1 rib.

2 Work in stocking stitch for 16 rows, or until work measures 4.5cm (1$^3/_4$in). Cast off.

TO SEW UP THE SWEATER

1 With a 6mm ($^1/_4$in) seam allowance, and right sides facing, sew the front to the back along one shoulder seam.

2 Sew in the sleeves, and then stitch the side seams.

3 Turn the right way out, put the sweater on the character, and slip stitch closed the remaining shoulder seam.

TROUSERS

1 Using tracing paper, make a copy of pattern no. 8 (see page 139).

2 Pin pattern to a double layer of fabric and cut out. With right sides together, and with a seam allowance of 6mm ($^1/_4$in), sew the two pieces together – up both sides and along the inner leg seams.

3 Put the trousers onto the character and secure with a couple of stitches to the soft body.

WAISTCOAT

1 Using tracing paper, make a copy of pattern no. 9 (see page 134).

2 Pin pattern to a double layer of fabric and cut out. With right sides together,

Step 3 Making the explorer's backpack

and with a seam allowance of 6mm ($^1/_4$in), sew the two pieces together – along the shoulder and side seams.

3 Fold the waistcoat in half, side seams together and crease. Unfold again and carefully cut straight up the foldline at the centre of the front of the jacket from the waist to the neckline.

4 Cut two or three tiny squares of fabric for the pockets and sew them onto the front.

BACKPACK

1 Using tracing paper, make a copy of pattern no. 12 (see page 135).

2 Cut out the shape for the backpack from a single thickness of fabric, and cut a curve at one end.

3 Stitch the bias binding all the way around the edge. Fold the fabric into three and hand sew up the sides to form a bag, leaving the curved part to form a flap at the front (*see photo above*).

4 Cut two lengths of bias binding to use as shoulder straps and secure them as loops to the back of the backpack with some firm stitches. Bring one of the explorer's arms through each loop and adjust the position of the backpack on the character's back, securing with a couple of stitches to the body if necessary.

Gardener Bear

• • • • • • • • • •

Gardener Bear sports a flat cap
and a pair of wellington boots.
There are simple instructions
on how to make his spade.

Actual size: height 15cm (6in)

Salt dough

75g (3oz) plain flour
40g (1½oz) table salt
40ml (1½fl oz or ³⁄₁₆ cup) water

In addition to your basic tools and equipment you will need:

Small paintbrush
Small sharp knife
Cocktail stick
2 small black beads for the eyes
1 hairpin cut to 25mm (1in)

Ready-made head base
(see Techniques page 9)
Drinking straw (medium-hole)
Fast-setting glue
Paints: brown, green, black and grey
30 x 7.5cm (12 x 3in) fabric
for the jacket
Small beads or buttons for the
front of the jacket
23 x 7.5cm (9 x 3in) fabric
for the trousers
Small amount of 4-ply knitting wool
Pair no. 3mm needles to knit the scarf

TO MAKE THE HEAD, ARMS AND LEGS

1 Roll a ball of dough the size of a golf ball for the head. Roll a marble-sized ball for the snout, roll it between your finger and thumb, and join it to the head. Smooth around the join with a damp paintbrush.

2 Roll out another piece of dough thinly, cut a small triangle, and join it to the end of the snout.

3 Roll a small ball of dough for the ears. Flatten it on a work surface and cut it in half. Curl the ears slightly forward, and join them to the head.

4 Make holes for the eyes with a cocktail stick. Wet these holes and push a bead into each eye socket.

5 Make the cap by rolling a small ball and flattening it between your finger and

thumb, keeping it a round shape. Make two holes for the ears, and join it to the head. With a sharp knife, separate the top of the cap from the peak at the front (*see photo overleaf*).

6 Push the hairpin into the lower part of the head under the chin to a depth of 13mm (½in), and position it in the head base with the rounded end of the hairpin in the centre opening.

7 To make the arms, roll a finger-sized rope of dough about 7.5cm (3in) long. Cut the rope in half and round off one end of each piece with your finger and thumb. Make three indentations in this rounded-off end with the knife to represent the paws. Using a drinking straw, make a hole 6mm (¼in) from the other end of the arm – at the shoulder.

Step 5 (page 101) Making the bear's cap

8 To make the legs and boots, roll another finger-sized rope of dough 11.5cm (4$\frac{1}{2}$in) long. Cut it in half, round off one end of each with your finger and thumb, and turn it up to form the boots.

9 Roll out a small piece of dough, cut it in half and fix the strips around the centre of the legs to make the tops of the boots (*see photo opposite*). Make a hole 6mm ($\frac{1}{4}$in) from the top of the legs with a drinking straw.

10 Place all the pieces onto a baking tray with the head and bake at 100°C (200°F or gas mark $\frac{1}{4}$) for about five hours.

11 When the dough has cooled, secure the hairpin in the head with a little fast-setting glue. Make hanging loops for each piece by threading some sewing cotton through the loop of the hairpin and through the holes in the arms and legs and tying it off.

12 When the baked dough has cooled, paint the head, arms and legs brown, and the nose and mouth black. Use grey for the cap, and green for the boots.

13 Apply two coats of varnish to all the dough parts.

14 To make the soft body, and to attach the head, arms and legs, see Techniques pages 10–11.

MAKING THE GARDENER BEAR'S CLOTHES

Step 9 (page 102) Making the bear's boots

JACKET

1 Using tracing paper, make a copy of pattern no. 7 (see page 139).

2 Pin the pattern to a double layer of fabric and cut out. With right sides facing, stitch the two pieces together along the shoulder, side and underarm seams with a 6mm ($^{1}/_{4}$in) seam allowance.

3 Fold the coat in half, side seams together and crease. Unfold again and carefully cut straight up the foldline at the centre of the front of the coat from the waist to the neckline.

4 Turn the coat the right way out and put it on the bear, securing it at the front with two buttons or beads.

SCARF

1 Cast on 22 stitches and work 12 rows in stocking stitch. Cast off.

2 Wrap the scarf around the bear's neck and slip stitch together the edges to form a seam at the back.

TROUSERS

1 Using tracing paper, make a copy of pattern no. 8 (see page 139).

2 Pin the pattern to a double layer of fabric and cut out. With right sides together, and with a 6mm ($^{1}/_{4}$in) seam allowance, stitch together the front and back pieces along the side and inner-leg seams.

Step 3 Making the bear's spade

3 Turn the trousers the right way out, put them on the bear and slip stitch the top of the trousers to the body around the waist.

4 Run a gathering stitch around the bottom of each trouser leg and adjust the gathers until the trouser leg fits snugly around the bear's leg.

MAKING THE SPADE

No gardener is complete without his spade. For this essential tool

you will need:
1 cocktail stick
Small amount of salt dough
Silver paint

1 Break or cut off the pointed end of the cocktail stick.

2 Roll out some dough to a thickness of $2\frac{1}{2}$mm ($\frac{1}{8}$in) and cut a tiny rectangle for the main blade.

3 Push one end of the cocktail stick into one end of the rectangle to act as the shaft (*see photo above*).

4 Roll a tiny rope of dough for the spade handle and join it to the opposite end of the stick.

5 Bake at 120°C (250°F or gas mark $\frac{1}{2}$) for about an hour.

Space Ranger

In his special spacesuit this space ranger makes a striking figure. You could make a simple space station out of corrugated cardboard sprayed silver for him to command.

Actual size: height 17.5cm (7in)

Salt dough

100g (4oz) plain flour

50g (2oz) table salt

50ml (2fl oz or $\frac{1}{4}$ cup) water

In addition to your basic tools and equipment you will need:

Round cutter 25mm (1in) in diameter

4 cocktail sticks

1 hairpin cut to 25mm (1in)

Ready-made head base (see Techniques page 9)

Small sharp knife

Drinking straw (medium-hole)

Fast-setting glue

Paints: pink, green, white, blue and silver

35.5 x 35.5cm (14 x 14in) stretch fabric (i.e. Lycra) for the all-in-one suit and

padded breastplate

35.5 x 5cm (14 x 2in) foam 6mm ($\frac{1}{4}$in thick for the inside of the padded breastplate

Scraps of green and silver fabric to decorate the suit

MAKING THE HEAD, ARMS AND LEGS

1 Roll a ball of dough the size of a golf ball for the head. Roll out some dough thinly and, with the round cutter, cut out the hat. Fix it to the head.

2 Roll four pea-sized balls of dough for the eyes and ears. Flatten the balls and join them to the head. With the cocktail stick, make holes for the eyes.

3 Roll out some more dough thinly and cut two narrow strips to make the goggles. Fix them around the eyes (see

photo overleaf). Make a nose from a tiny flattened ball, and join it to the head.

4 Make a hole for the mouth with the cocktail stick.

5 Push the hairpin into the lower part of the head under the chin to a depth of 13mm ($\frac{1}{2}$in), and position it in the head base with the rounded end of the hairpin in the centre opening.

6 To make the gloves, roll a thick rope of dough about 10cm (4in) long. Cut the

Step 3 (page 107) Making the space ranger's goggles

rope in half and round off one end of each piece with your finger and thumb. Press your finger into the centre of the non-rounded ends and pull up the edges to make a point at one side (*see photo below*). Cut some fingers for the gloves with a knife.

7 To make the upper arms, roll another thinner rope of dough, 5cm (2in) long, and cut it in half. Break or cut off the ends of two cocktail sticks, and push them down into the indented tops of the gloves, leaving about 13mm (¹/₂in) sticking out. Push the ends of the upper arms onto the sticks to join the arms to the gloves.

Step 4 (page 107) Making the space ranger's gloves

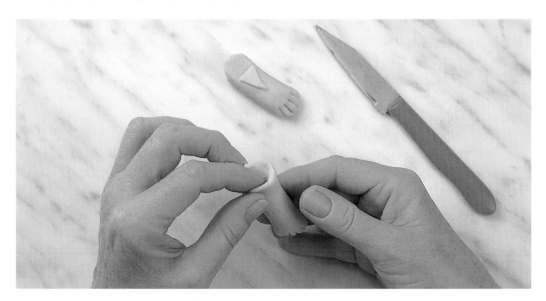

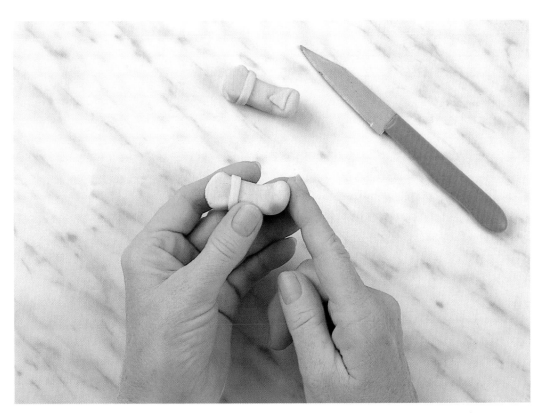

Step 10 Making the space ranger's boots

8 Roll out some dough thinly, cut out two triangles, and join them to the gloves. Using a drinking straw, make a hole 6mm (¹/₄in) from the other end of the arm – at the shoulder.

9 To make the legs and boots, roll two more ropes of dough: one should be a thick rope 10cm (4in) long, and the other, for the legs, should be finger-thick and 7.5cm (3in) long. Cut both in half.

10 Take the bigger boot pieces, round off one end of each piece and turn it upwards (*see photo above*). Press your finger into the centre of the top of the boots and pull up the front and back.

11 Break off the ends of two cocktail sticks, and push them down the centre hole of the boots, leaving about 13mm (¹/₂in) sticking out. Push the ends of the legs onto the sticks to join them to the boots.

12 Roll a thin rope of dough and two triangles as before and stick to the boots. With a drinking straw, make a hole 6mm (¹/₄in) from the top of the legs.

13 Place all the pieces onto a baking tray with the head and bake at 120°C (240°F or gas mark ¹/₂) for about four hours.

14 When the dough has cooled, secure the hairpin in the head with a little fast-setting glue. Make hanging loops for each piece by threading some sewing cotton through the loop of the hairpin and through the holes in the arms and legs and tying it off.

15 When the baked dough is cool, use pink, white, blue and green to paint the face. The goggles should be silver and the gloves and boots white, decorated with silver and green.

16 Apply two coats of varnish to all the dough pieces.

17 To make the soft body, and to attach the head, arms and legs, see Techniques pages 10–11.

MAKING THE SPACE RANGER'S CLOTHES

ALL-IN-ONE SUIT

1 Using tracing paper, make a copy of pattern no. 15 (see page 142).

2 Pin pattern to a double layer of fabric and cut out. With right sides facing, stitch the two pieces together along the shoulder, side and underarm and inner leg seams with a 6mm (1/4in) seam allowance.

3 Fold the suit in half, side seams together and crease. Unfold again and, taking the back panel, carefully cut 25mm (1in) down the centre foldline from the neckline.

4 Dress the space ranger in his suit and glue the ends of the sleeves and trouser legs to the inside of the gloves and boots. Slip stitch closed the back opening.

PADDED BREASTPLATE

1 Using tracing paper, make a copy of pattern no. 17 (see page 142).

2 Pin the pattern to a double layer of fabric and cut out. With right sides together, and with a seam allowance of 6mm (1/4in), sew the two pieces together where indicated. Turn the right way out.

3 Cut out the same shape from a single thickness of foam padding. Push it between the two halves of the top. Slip stitch closed the side which is open.

4 Put the top onto the space ranger and slip stitch together the front and back panels at the shoulder seams.

5 Cut two triangles in fabric and a small belt. Glue the triangles to the front of the padded top, and tie the belt around the waist.

Wise Wizard

. . . .

This wise old wizard makes an interesting character with his dramatic cloak and long, white beard. You can just imagine him casting spells and concocting magic potions.

Actual size: height 17.5cm (7in)

Salt dough

75g (3oz) plain flour

40g (1$\frac{1}{2}$oz) table salt

40ml (1$\frac{1}{2}$fl oz or $\frac{3}{16}$ cup) water

In addition to your basic tools and equipment you will need:

Drinking straw (medium-hole)

1 hairpin cut to 25mm (1in)

Cocktail stick

Small sharp knife

Fast-setting glue

Paints: red, black and silver

66 x 11cm (26 x 4$\frac{1}{2}$in) black fabric for the cloak, dress and hat

30 x 11cm (12 x 4$\frac{1}{2}$in) contrasting fabric to line the cloak

Kitchen foil to make the stars and moons for the cloak

Small amount of fibre filling to make the hair and beard

MAKING THE HEAD, ARMS, LEGS AND BOOTS

1 Roll a ball of dough the size of a table tennis ball for the head. Pinch out the nose. Make holes for the eyes and mouth with a cocktail stick.

2 Push the hairpin into the lower part of the head under the chin to a depth of 13mm ($\frac{1}{2}$in).

3 To make the arms and hands, roll a finger-sized rope of dough 10cm (4in) long. Cut it in half and round off one end of each piece with your finger and thumb. Cut some fingers in the rounded ends. Make a hole 6mm ($\frac{1}{4}$in) in from the tops of the arms with the drinking straw.

4 To make the legs and boots: roll another rope of dough 7.5cm (3in) long and cut it in half. Then roll two balls the size of large marbles for the boots. Roll them slightly in the palm of your hand and make a point at one end. With your finger, make a hole in the centre of each boot and draw up the sides and back, trimming off any excess dough with your knife.

5 Make a small cut in the front of the shoe and turn out the corners. Wet the inside of each boot and join them to the legs. Make a hole 6mm ($\frac{1}{4}$in) in from the tops of the legs with a drinking straw (*see photo overleaf*).

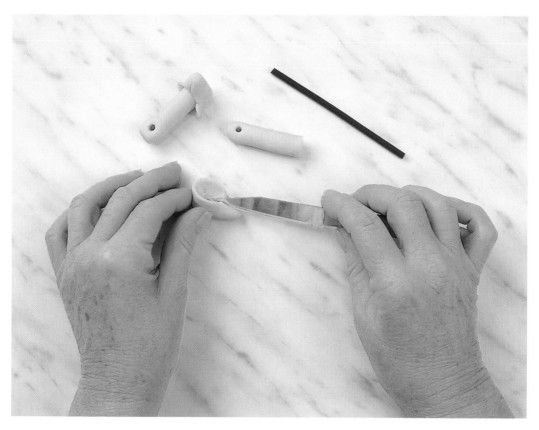

Step 5 (page 113) Making the wizard's boots

6 Place all the pieces onto a baking tray and bake at 120°C (240°F or gas mark $\frac{1}{2}$) for about four hours.

7 When the dough has cooled, secure the hairpin in the head with a little fast-setting glue. Make hanging loops for each piece by threading some sewing cotton through the loop of the hairpin and through the holes in the arms and legs and tying it off.

8 When the baked dough is cool, paint the cheeks a watery red and the legs black. Use silver for the boots.

9 Apply two coats of varnish to all the dough pieces.

10 To make the soft body, and to attach the head, arms and legs, see Techniques pages 10–11.

11 To finish the head, stretch the fibre filling with your fingers to make the hair and beard, and using glue, attach the hair to the head and make a beard around the chin.

MAKING THE WIZARD'S CLOTHES

ROBE

1 Using tracing paper, make a copy of pattern no. 13 (see page 138).

2 Using a double thickness of fabric, cut out pattern no.13 for the robe. Stitch the two shorter sides together.

3 Turn over and stitch a 13mm ($\frac{1}{2}$in) hem at one end of the robe.

4 Run a gathering stitch across the other end, leave the ends loose.

5 Put the robe onto the wizard and pull the gathering threads to fit around the neck. Secure the ends of the gathering threads.

6 With scissors, cut two holes in the fabric to let the hands show through.

CAPE

1 Use pattern no. 13 again for the cape (see page 138).

2 Lay a double thickness of fabric on a double thickness of lining, pin the pattern on the two layers of fabric and cut out.

3 With the right side of the fabric facing the right side of the lining, and with a 6mm ($\frac{1}{4}$in) seam allowance, sew around the three sides of the cape.

4 Turn the cape the right way out and press it.

5 Run a gathering stitch around the top of the cape leaving the thread loose.

6 Put the cape around the wizard and adjust the gathers to fit the neck. Cast off.

7 For a finishing touch, cut out some stars and moons from the kitchen foil and glue them to the cape.

HAT

1 Using tracing paper, make a copy of pattern no. 11 (see page 134).

2 Using a double thickness of fabric, cut out pattern no. 11 for the hat.

3 With right sides together and with a 6mm ($\frac{1}{4}$in) seam allowance, stitch together the sides.

4 Turn the hat the right way out and glue the hat to the head.

5 To finish the hat, cut out some stars and moons from the kitchen foil and glue them to it.

Pirate Pig

● ● ● ● ● ● ● ● ● ● ●

You'll enjoy making this

swashbuckling character with

his eyepatch, wooden leg

and parrot.

Actual size: height 15cm (6in)

Salt dough

50g (2oz) plain flour

25g (1oz) table salt

25ml (1fl oz or $\frac{1}{8}$ cup) water

In addition to your basic tools and equipment you will need

Small sharp knife

Cocktail stick

1 small black bead for the eye

1 hairpin cut to 25mm (1in)

Drinking straw (medium-hole)

Fast-setting glue

Paints: black and pink

Piece of wood (the end of a pencil can be used) 25mm (1in) long

30 x 7.5cm (12 x 3in) fabric for the shirt

1 small black bead to fasten the shirt

23 x 7.5cm (9 x 3in) fabric for the trousers

12.5 x 12.5cm (5 x 5in) for the head scarf

Oddments of fabric to make the sash for the waist and neck scarf

MAKING THE HEAD, ARMS AND LEGS

1 Roll a ball of dough the size of a golf ball for the head. Roll a small rope about the thickness of a finger, cut from it a piece 13mm ($\frac{1}{8}$in) long, and join that to the head for the snout.

2 Make holes in the end of the snout with a cocktail stick.

3 Make a hole for one eye with a cocktail stick, wet the hole and push a bead into the eye socket.

4 Make the patch for the other eye from a thin rope of dough and a tiny flattened ball of dough. Attach the patch in place of the other eye and run the rope around the pirate's head (*see photo opposite*).

5 Take two tiny balls of dough for the ears, roll them into ropes and then squeeze them into pig's ear shapes. Join these quite high on the head.

6 Push the hairpin into the lower part of the head under the chin to a depth of 13mm ($\frac{1}{2}$in) and place it onto the head base, with the rounded end of the hairpin sitting in the centre opening.

7 To make the arms, roll a finger-sized rope of dough about 7.5cm (3in) long. Cut the rope in half and cut a notch at one end of each arm for the trotters. At the shoulder end, make a hole 6mm ($\frac{1}{4}$in) from the top, with a drinking straw.

8 To make the legs (1 real and 1 wooden), roll another rope of dough 10cm (4in) long. Cut it in half and cut a notch at the end of the leg that will be the real one. Cut the other leg in half, and push the stick into it, leaving visible about 20mm ($\frac{3}{4}$in) (*see photo overleaf*). With a drinking straw, make a hole 6mm ($\frac{1}{4}$in) from the tops of the legs.

9 Place all the pieces on a baking tray and bake at 100°C (200°F or gas mark $\frac{1}{4}$) for about five hours.

10 When the dough has cooled, secure the hairpin in the head with a little fast-setting glue. Make hanging loops for each piece by threading some sewing cotton through the loop of the hairpin and through the holes in the arms and legs and tying it off.

11 When the baked dough is cool, paint the head, arms and legs pink. When the pink is dry paint the patch black,

12 Apply two coats of varnish to all the pieces.

13 To make the soft body, and to attach the head, arms and legs, see Techniques pages 10–11.

Step 4 (page 118) Making the pig's eye patch

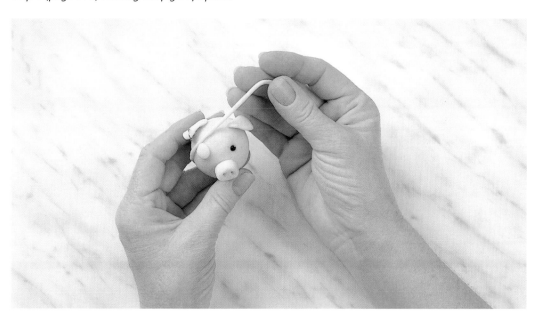

Step 8 (page 119) Making the pirate pig's wooden leg

MAKING THE PIRATE PIG'S CLOTHES

SHIRT

1 Using tracing paper, make a copy of pattern no. 7 (see page 139).

2 Pin pattern to a double layer of fabric and cut out. With right sides facing, stitch the two pieces together along the shoulder, side and underarm seams with a 6mm ($^1/_4$in) seam allowance.

3 Fold the jacket in half, side seams together, and crease. Unfold again and carefully cut straight up the foldline at the centre of the front of the shirt from the waist to the neckline.

4 Turn the shirt the right way out, put it on the pirate, fold the two shirt fronts over one another and secure by sewing a bead halfway up the front.

TROUSERS

1 Using tracing paper, make a copy of pattern no. 8 (see page 139).

2 Pin pattern to a double layer of fabric and cut out. Then cut 25mm (1in) off one of the legs.

3 With right sides together, and with a seam allowance of 6mm ($^1/_4$in), sew the two pieces together – up both sides and along the inner leg seams.

4 Turn the trousers the right way out, put onto the pirate pig and secure with a couple of stitches to the body.

Step1 Making the pirate pig's parrot

FINISHING

1 Tie the scraps of fabric around his waist and neck.

2 Fold in half the square of fabric you have for the headscarf and, with scissors, make holes each side for the ears. Tie it around the head and bring the ears through.

3 Sew the parrot (see below for instructions) to the pirate's shoulder.

TO MAKE THE PARROT

you will need:
. . . .

Salt dough

1 hairpin

Paints: red, blue, yellow, green and black

Fast-setting glue

Small scissors

1 Roll a small rope of dough and squeeze the tail end. Using the scissors, cut the dough to indicate the wings and some feathers (*see photo above*).

2 Pinch the dough to form the beak and hook it slightly. Cut the rounded part of the hairpin to 6mm ($\frac{1}{2}$in) and press it into the parrot's chest leaving visible a tiny eyelet – to sew it on to the pirate's shirt.

3 Bake the parrot with the pirate. When the baked dough is cool, secure the eyelet with a few drops of the fast setting glue. Then paint and varnish.

Super Hero Mouse

● ● ● ● ● ● ● ● ● ● ●

This character looks like a super hero with his mask, cape and initials on his skin-tight suit. You can just imagine him flying across the roof tops on a mission to save someone.

Actual size: height 15cm (6in)

Salt dough

50g (2oz) plain flour

25g (1oz) table salt

25ml (1fl oz or $\frac{1}{8}$ cup) water

In addition to your basic tools and equipment you will need:

Cocktail stick

1 small black bead for the nose

2 black stamens for the whiskers (available from craft shops)

1 hairpin cut to 25mm (1in)

Ready-made head base (see Techniques page 9)

Small sharp knife

Drinking straw (medium-hole)

Fast-setting glue

Paint: grey, black, red and white

25.5 x 28cm (10 x 11in) stretch fabric i.e. Lycra to make the all-in-one suit

20.5 x 13cm (8 x 5in) stretch fabric i.e. Lycra in contrasting colour to make leotard

16.5 x 10cm (6$\frac{1}{2}$ x 4in) in two contrasting colours to make the cape

TO MAKE THE HEAD, ARMS AND LEGS

1 Roll a ball of dough the size of a golf ball, and pinch out one piece for the nose. Make a hole at the end of the nose with a cocktail stick. Wet the hole and push in a black bead.

2 Make the ears from two small, flattened balls of dough, curl them slightly and fix them to the head.

3 Roll a tiny rope of dough to make the mask. Make two rings and fix them to the front first (see photo opposite), then add the central piece between, and then a strap that runs around the back of the head. Use the cocktail stick to make holes for the eyes.

4 Cut the stamens into six lengths. Push the ends into either side of the nose to act as whiskers. Add a tiny piece of dough for the teeth.

Step 3 (page 124) Making the mouse mask

5 Push the hairpin into the lower part of the head under the chin to a depth of 13mm ($\frac{1}{2}$in) and place it onto the head base, with the rounded end of the hairpin sitting in the centre opening.

6 To make the arms, roll a finger-sized rope of dough about 7.5cm (3in) long. Cut the rope in half and round off one end of each arm with your finger and thumb. Using a drinking straw, make a hole 6mm ($\frac{1}{4}$in) from the other end of the arm – at the shoulder.

7 To make the legs and shoes, roll another rope of dough 10cm (4in) long and cut it in half. Roll two small marble-sized balls of dough for the shoes. Make an indentation in the top of the shoes with your finger, wet the holes and join the legs to the shoes. With a drinking straw, make a hole 6mm ($\frac{1}{4}$in) from the tops of the legs.

8 Place the head, arms and legs onto a baking tray and bake at 120°C (240°F or gas mark $\frac{1}{2}$) for about four hours.

9 When the dough has cooled put some fast-setting glue around the holes of the hairpin, to keep it in place.

10 Thread some sewing cotton through the hole of the hairpin and holes in the arms and legs and tie it off to make hanging loops for each piece.

11 When the baked dough is cool, paint the head, arms and legs grey, the teeth white, and the inside of the ears pink. Use red for the shoes. When the grey is dry use black for the mask, paws and eyes.

12 Apply two coats of varnish to all the dough pieces.

13 To make the soft body, and to attach the head, arms and legs, see Techniques pages 10–11.

MAKING THE CLOTHES FOR SUPER HERO MOUSE

ALL-IN-ONE SUIT

1 Using tracing paper, make a copy of pattern no. 15 (see page 142).

2 Pin pattern to a double layer of fabric and cut out. With right sides facing, stitch the two pieces together along the shoulder, side and underarm and inner leg seams with a 6mm ($\frac{1}{4}$in) seam allowance.

3 Fold the suit in half, side seams together and crease. Unfold again and, taking the back panel, carefully cut 25mm (1in) down the centre foldline from the neckline. Turn the right way out.

4 Dress the super hero in his suit and slip stitch closed the back opening.

LEOTARD

1 Using tracing paper, make a copy of pattern no. 16 (see page 137).

2 Pin pattern to a double layer of fabric and cut out. With right sides facing, stitch the two pieces together along the shoulder, side and crotch seams with a 6mm ($\frac{1}{4}$in) seam allowance.

3 Turn the right way out and put the leotard on the mouse, over the suit.

4 Cut a thin strip of fabric from the cape allowance and make a belt.

5 Cut the letters 'S' and 'M' from felt fabric and glue them to the front of the leotard.

CAPE

1 Using tracing paper, make a copy of pattern no. 14 (see page 140).

2 Lay a single thickness of fabric on another single thickness of contrasting fabric, pin the pattern on the two layers of fabric and cut out.

3 With right sides together, and with a 6mm ($\frac{1}{4}$in) seam allowance, stitch together where indicated.

4 Turn the cape the right way out and press it.

5 Run a gathering stitch around the top of the cape leaving the thread loose.

6 Put the cape around the mouse's shoulders and adjust the gathers to fit the neck. Secure the ends of the gathering threads.

Jogger

· · · · · · · · · · ·

With this character you will
see how to make a personal
stereo, cap and tracksuit.

Actual size: height 15cm (6in)

Salt dough

75g (3oz) plain flour

40g (1½oz) table salt

40ml (1½fl oz or ³⁄₁₆ cup) water

In addition to your basic tools and equipment you will need:

Cocktail stick

Garlic press

Small sharp knife

1 hairpin cut to 25mm (1in)

Ready-made head base (see Techniques page 9)

Fast-setting glue

Paints: red, white, brown and blue

56 x 20cm (22 x 8in) for the tracksuit

Oddment of fabric to trim the tracksuit (contrasting colour)

TO MAKE THE HEAD, ARMS AND LEGS

1 Roll a ball of dough the size of a golf ball for the head. Roll a smaller ball and press your finger into the centre to make the hat.

2 Make holes for the eyes and mouth with a cocktail stick. Roll a tiny ball for the nose and join it to the head.

3 Push some dough through a garlic press to make some hair, and join it to the head.

4 Roll out some dough thinly and cut a small peak for the front of the cap, and fix it on the head (*see photo below*).

Step 4 Making the jogger's cap

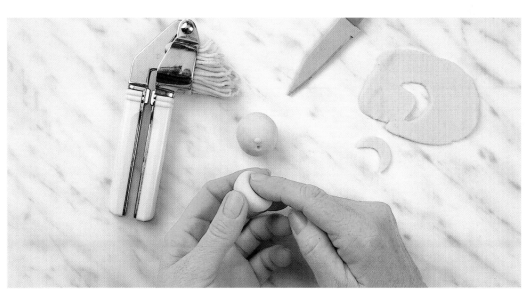

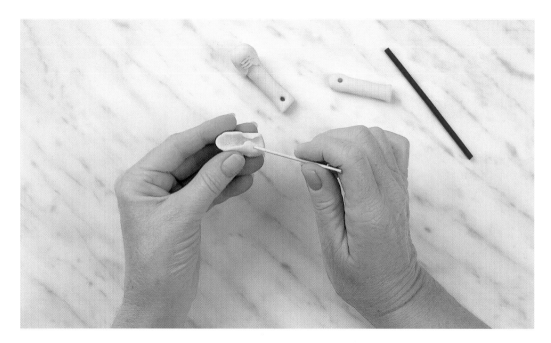

Step 10 Making the jogger's trainers

5 Using two small, flattened balls and a thinly rolled rope of dough, make the earphones and headpiece for the personal stereo. Join them to the head.

6 Push the hairpin into the lower part of the head under the chin to a depth of about 13mm ($^1/_2$in), and place the head onto the ready-made head base with the rounded end of the hairpin in the centre opening.

7 To make the arms, roll a finger-sized rope of dough 9cm (3$^1/_2$in) long. Cut it in half and flatten one end of each piece with your finger and thumb to form the hands. Cut some fingers with a knife. Make a hole 6mm (¼in) in from the tops of the arms with the drinking straw.

8 To make the legs, roll another rope of dough 9cm (3$^1/_2$in) long. Cut it in half, and make a hole 6mm ($^1/_4$in) from the top of the legs with the drinking straw. Then put aside under a teacloth while you make the trainers.

9 To make the trainers, roll two balls of dough the size of large marbles. Roll them into an oval shape. With your finger, make a hole slightly off-centre towards the back of each shoe. Draw up the two top side pieces of the shoes, and bring them towards the centre of the trainer.

10 With a cocktail stick, make holes for the laces on each side (*see photo above*). Roll a tiny rope for the laces, cut these into tiny lengths and join them to the trainers. Take out the legs again, wet the bottom end of each leg, and join them to the trainers.

11 Place all the pieces onto a baking tray and bake at 120°C (240°F or gas mark $\frac{1}{2}$) for about four hours.

12 When the dough has cooled, secure the hairpin in the head with a little fast-setting glue. Make hanging loops for each piece by threading some sewing cotton through the loop of the hairpin and through the holes in the arms and legs and tying it off.

13 When the baked dough is cool, paint the cap and the eyes blue. Use red, black and white for the training shoes and black for the personal stereo.

14 Apply two coats of varnish to all dough parts.

15 To make the soft body, and to attach the head, arms and legs, see Techniques pages 10–11.

MAKING THE JOGGER'S TRACKSUIT

TRACKSUIT TOP

1 Using tracing paper, make a copy of pattern no. 7 (see page 139).

2 Pin pattern to a double layer of fabric and cut out. With right sides facing, stitch the two pieces together along the shoulder, side and underarm seams with a 6mm ($\frac{1}{4}$in) seam allowance.

3 Fold the top in half, side seams together and crease. Unfold again and, taking the front panel, carefully cut up the centre foldline from the waist to the neckline.

4 Turn the right way out and dress the jogger in his tracksuit top. Slip stitch closed the front opening.

5 Run a gathering stitch around the end of the sleeves and pull the thread to gather it tightly around the wrists. Cast off.

TRACKSUIT BOTTOMS

1 Using tracing paper, make a copy of pattern no. 8 (see page 139).

2 Pin the pattern to a double layer of fabric and cut out. With right sides together, and with a seam allowance of 6mm ($\frac{1}{4}$in), sew the two pieces together – up both sides and along the inner leg seams.

3 Turn the bottoms the right way out, put onto the jogger and slip stitch the top of the tracksuit bottoms to the soft body to keep them in place.

4 Run a gathering stitch around the ends of the bottoms, and adjust the gathers to fit snugly at the ankles. Cast off.

For a really professional finish, glue lengths of narrow ribbon from the neckline down the arms of the top and down the outside side seams of the bottoms.

Patterns

The following chapter features
all the patterns you need to
make the different characters'
clothes and accessories. In each
project there are step-by-step
instructions on tracing and
cutting out them out.

PATTERN NO. 9
WAISTCOAT

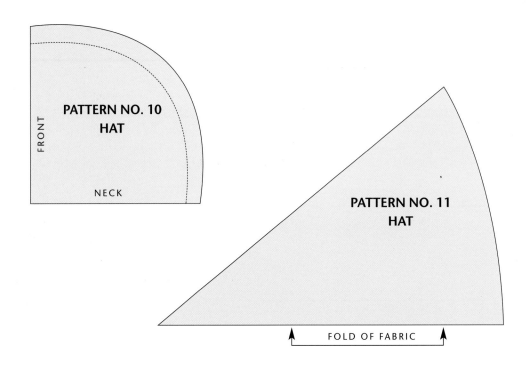

PATTERN NO. 10
HAT

FRONT

NECK

PATTERN NO. 11
HAT

FOLD OF FABRIC

FOLD

**PATTERN NO. 12
BACKPACK**

FOLD

TOP FLAP

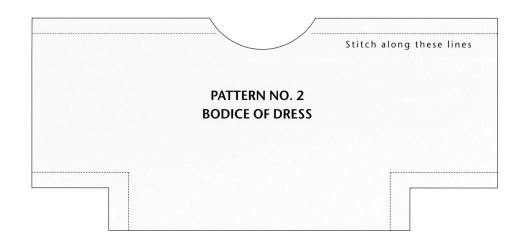

Stitch along these lines

**PATTERN NO. 2
BODICE OF DRESS**

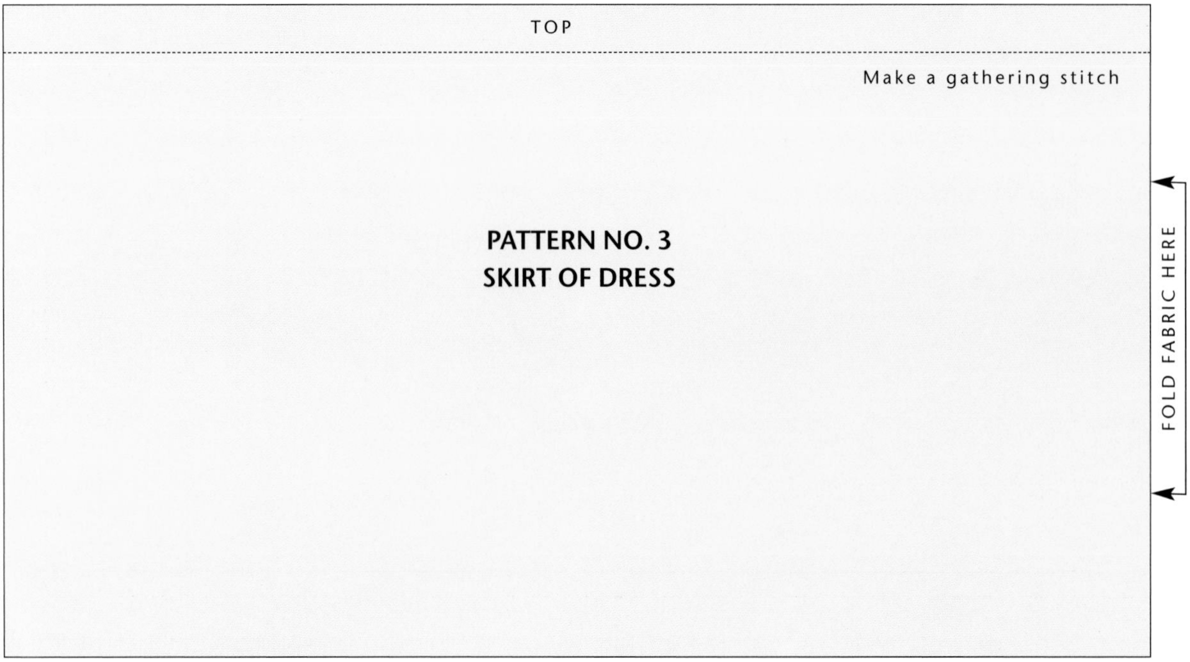

TOP

Make a gathering stitch

PATTERN NO. 3
SKIRT OF DRESS

FOLD FABRIC HERE

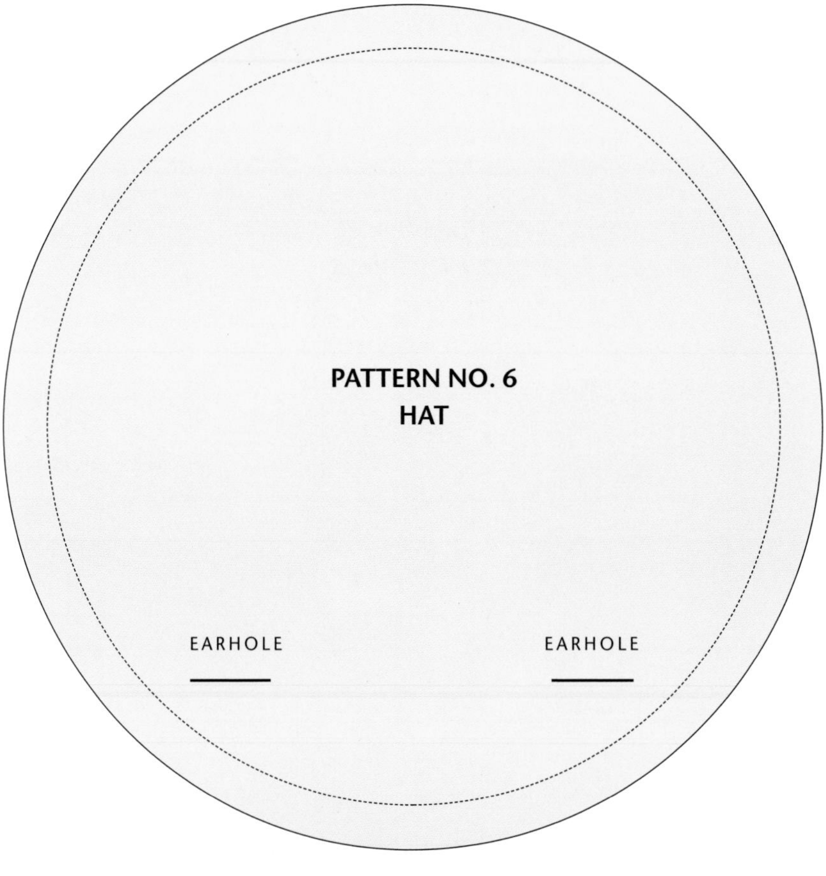

PATTERN NO. 6
HAT

EARHOLE

EARHOLE

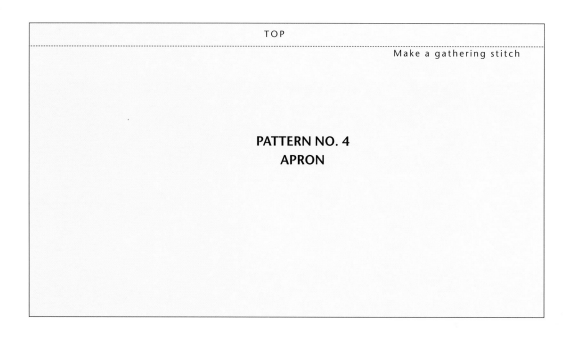

TOP

Make a gathering stitch

**PATTERN NO. 4
APRON**

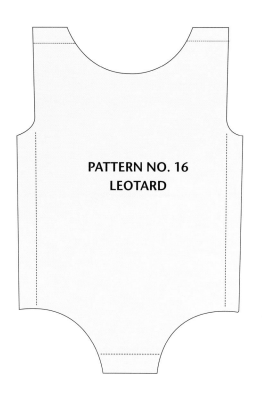

**PATTERN NO. 16
LEOTARD**

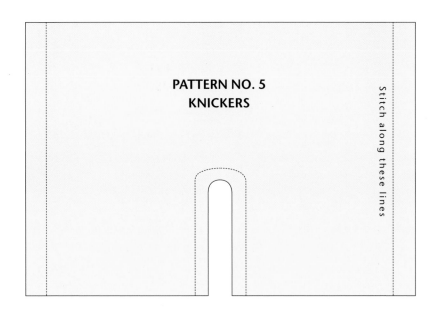

**PATTERN NO. 5
KNICKERS**

Stitch along these lines

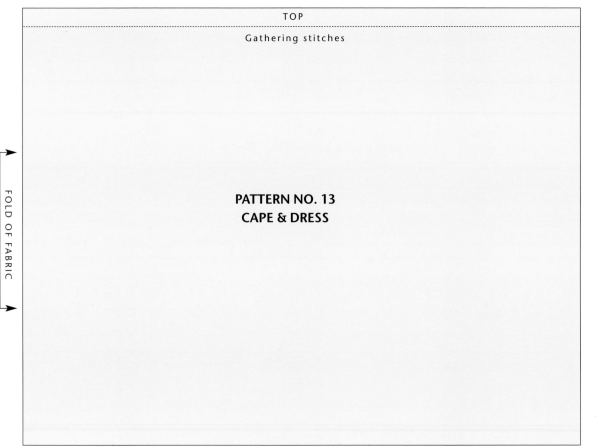

TOP

Gathering stitches

**PATTERN NO. 13
CAPE & DRESS**

FOLD OF FABRIC

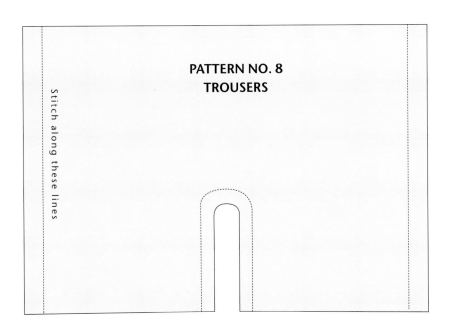

**PATTERN NO. 8
TROUSERS**

Stitch along these lines

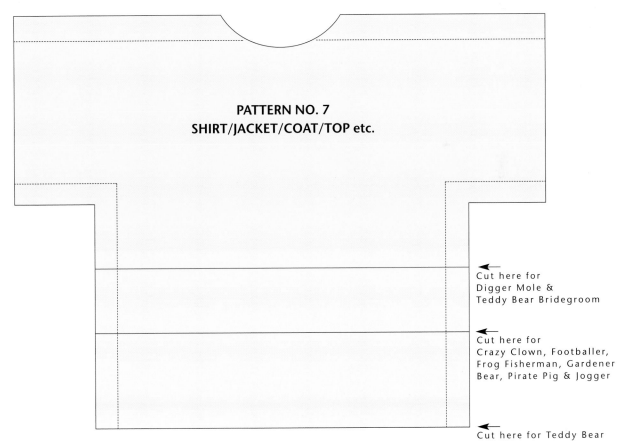

**PATTERN NO. 7
SHIRT/JACKET/COAT/TOP etc.**

← Cut here for
Digger Mole &
Teddy Bear Bridegroom

← Cut here for
Crazy Clown, Footballer,
Frog Fisherman, Gardener
Bear, Pirate Pig & Jogger

← Cut here for Teddy Bear

**TEMPLATE
WINGS FOR THE ANGEL**

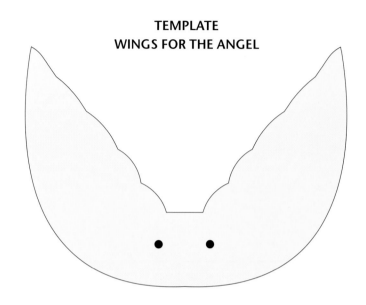

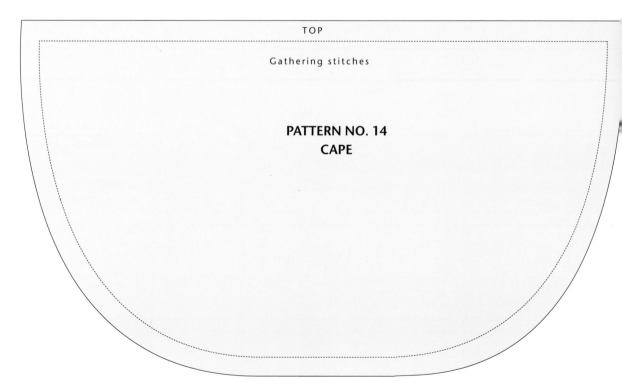

TOP

Gathering stitches

**PATTERN NO. 14
CAPE**

Stitch along these lines

**PATTERN NO. 1
DRESS FOR THE ANGEL**

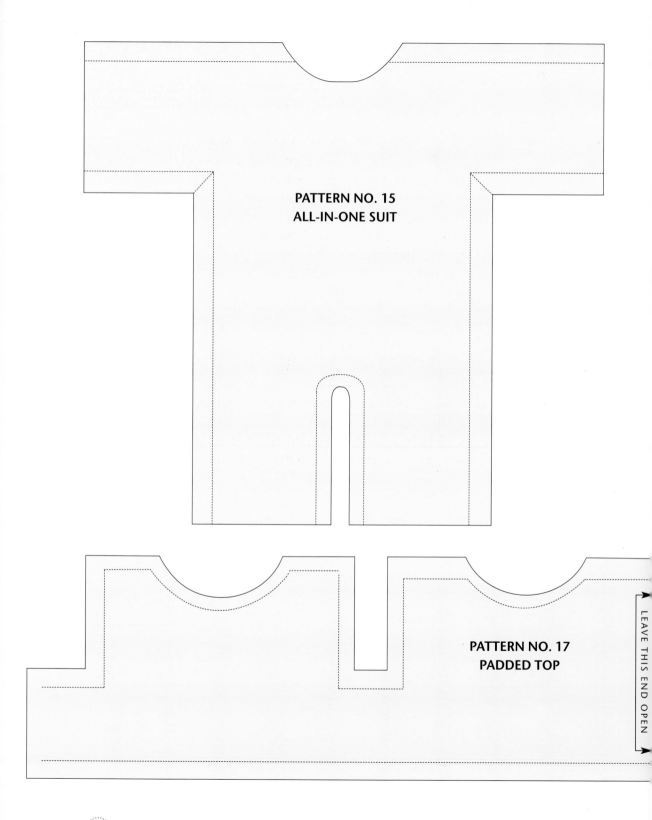

PATTERN NO. 15
ALL-IN-ONE SUIT

PATTERN NO. 17
PADDED TOP

LEAVE THIS END OPEN

ABOUT THE AUTHOR

Patricia Hughes has followed a career as an accomplished interior designer, possessing many qualifications in this subject. She has always had a creative mind and has explored many other aspects of art. This is her second published book on doughcraft in which she hopes to further inspire readers to take up this wonderful craft. *Creative Doughcraft* is also published by GMC Publications.

ACKNOWLEDGEMENTS

My thanks to my husband, Anthony, for his never-ending support. Thanks also to my daughters, Amanda and Natalie, and my sisters, Isabel, Rosemary and Mary for all their encouragement and support.

Woodturning Jewellery — Hilary Bowen
Woodturning Masterclass — Tony Boase
Woodturning Techniques — GMC Publications
Woodturning Tools & Equipment Test Reports — GMC Publications
Woodturning Wizardry — David Springett

WOODWORKING

Bird Boxes and Feeders for the Garden — Dave Mackenzie
Complete Woodfinishing — Ian Hosker
David Charlesworth's Furniture-Making Techniques — David Charlesworth
Furniture & Cabinetmaking Projects — GMC Publications
Furniture-Making Projects for the Wood Craftsman — GMC Publications
Furniture-Making Techniques for the Wood Craftsman — GMC Publications
Furniture Projects — Rod Wales
Furniture Restoration (Practical Crafts) — Kevin Jan Bonner
Furniture Restoration and Repair for Beginners — Kevin Jan Bonner
Furniture Restoration Workshop — Kevin Jan Bonner
Green Woodwork — Mike Abbott
Kevin Ley's Furniture Projects — Kevin Ley
Making & Modifying Woodworking Tools — Jim Kingshott
Making Chairs and Tables — GMC Publications
Making Classic English Furniture — Paul Richardson
Making Little Boxes from Wood — John Bennett
Making Shaker Furniture — Barry Jackson
Making Woodwork Aids and Devices — Robert Wearing
Minidrill: Fifteen Projects — John Everett
Pine Furniture Projects for the Home — Dave Mackenzie
Router Magic: Jigs, Fixtures and Tricks to Unleash your Router's Full Potential — Bill Hylton
Routing for Beginners — Anthony Bailey
Scrollsaw Pattern Book — John Everett
Scrollsaw Projects — GMC Publications
The Scrollsaw: Twenty Projects — John Everett
Sharpening: The Complete Guide — Jim Kingshott

Sharpening Pocket Reference Book — Jim Kingshott
Space-Saving Furniture Projects — Dave Mackenzie
Stickmaking: A Complete Course — Andrew Jones & Clive George
Stickmaking Handbook — Andrew Jones & Clive George
Test Reports: The Router and Furniture & Cabinetmaking — GMC Publications
Veneering: A Complete Course — Ian Hosker
Woodfinishing Handbook (Practical Crafts) — Ian Hosker
Woodworking with the Router: Professional Router Techniques any Woodworker can Use — Bill Hylton & Fred Matlack
The Workshop — Jim Kingshott

UPHOLSTERY

The Upholsterer's Pocket Reference Book — David James
Upholstery: A Complete Course (Revised Edition) — David James
Upholstery Restoration — David James
Upholstery Techniques & Projects — David James
Upholstery Tips and Hints — David James

TOYMAKING

Designing & Making Wooden Toys — Terry Kelly
Fun to Make Wooden Toys & Games — Jeff & Jennie Loader
Restoring Rocking Horses — Clive Green & Anthony Dew
Scrollsaw Toy Projects — Ivor Carlyle
Scrollsaw Toys for All Ages — Ivor Carlyle
Wooden Toy Projects — GMC Publications

DOLLS' HOUSES AND MINIATURES

Architecture for Dolls' Houses — Joyce Percival
A Beginners' Guide to the Dolls' House Hobby — Jean Nisbett
The Complete Dolls' House Book — Jean Nisbett
The Dolls' House 1/24 Scale: A Complete Introduction — Jean Nisbett
Dolls' House Accessories, Fixtures and Fittings — Andrea Barham

CRAFTS

Tatting Collage   *Lindsay Rogers*
Temari: A Traditional Japanese Embroidery
   Technique   *Margaret Ludlow*
Theatre Models in Paper and Card
                     Robert Burgess
Wool Embroidery and Design   *Lee Lockheed*

Woodturning: A Foundation Course
                     Keith Rowley
Carving a Figure: The Female Form
                     Ray Gonzalez
The Router: A Beginner's Guide   *Alan Goodsell*
The Scroll Saw: A Beginner's Guide   *John Burke*

GARDENING

Auriculas for Everyone: How to Grow and
   Show Perfect Plants   *Mary Robinson*
Bird Boxes and Feeders for the Garden
                     Dave Mackenzie
The Birdwatcher's Garden
               Hazel & Pamela Johnson
Broad-Leaved Evergreens   *Stephen G. Haw*
Companions to Clematis: Growing Clematis
   with Other Plants   *Marigold Badcock*
Creating Contrast with Dark Plants *Freya Martin*
Gardening with Wild Plants   *Julian Slatcher*
Hardy Perennials: A Beginner's Guide
                     Eric Sawford
The Living Tropical Greenhouse: Creating
   a Haven for Butterflies
               John & Maureen Tampion
Orchids are Easy: A Beginner's Guide to their
Care and Cultivation   *Tom Gilland*
Plants that Span the Seasons   *Roger Wilson*

VIDEOS

Drop-in and Pinstuffed Seats   *David James*
Stuffover Upholstery   *David James*
Elliptical Turning   *David Springett*
Woodturning Wizardry   *David Springett*
Turning Between Centres: The Basics
                     Dennis White
Turning Bowls   *Dennis White*
Boxes, Goblets and Screw Threads *Dennis White*
Novelties and Projects   *Dennis White*
Classic Profiles   *Dennis White*
Twists and Advanced Turning   *Dennis White*
Sharpening the Professional Way   *Jim Kingshott*
Sharpening Turning & Carving Tools
                     Jim Kingshott
Bowl Turning   *John Jordan*
Hollow Turning   *John Jordan*

MAGAZINES

WOODTURNING

WOODCARVING

FURNITURE & CABINETMAKING

THE ROUTER

WOODWORKING

THE DOLLS' HOUSE MAGAZINE

WATER GARDENING

EXOTIC GARDENING

GARDEN CALENDAR

OUTDOOR PHOTOGRAPHY

BUSINESSMATTERS

The above represents a full list of all titles
currently published or scheduled to be
published.
All are available direct from the Publishers
or through bookshops, newsagents and
specialist retailers.
To place an order, or to obtain a complete
catalogue, contact:

**GMC Publications,
Castle Place,
166 High Street, Lewes,
East Sussex BN7 1XU,
United Kingdom
Tel: 01273 488005
Fax: 01273 478606
E-mail: pubs@thegmcgroup.com**
Orders by credit card are accepted

BY THE SAME AUTHOR

This ever popular popular craft is versatile, colourful and easy to master. Exciting doughcraft can be achieved with just a few simple, cheap ingredients and tools. Fully-illustrated instructions and a wealth of handy hints ensure that everyone, adults and children alike, can produce stunning gifts and decorative items for the home.

All the basics are covered in detail including:

- RECIPES FOR SALT DOUGH AND BREAD DOUGH
- BASIC TECHNIQUES
- MAKING SIMPLE SHAPES
- ADVICE ON PAINTS, VARNISHES AND PROBLEM SOLVING

Bread dough, unlike salt dough, can be used to create fine, delicate work. By combining bread dough with salt dough the author creates colourful, robust and intricate items. Easy-to-follow steps, with full colour photographs, will guide the reader through a variety of projects including:

- SUNFLOWER GARLAND • BASKET OF ROSES • THREE DUCKS OUT FOR A WALK • HEART AND DOVE MOBILE • FLOWER BALL IN A PLANT POT • SUN AND BUMBLE BEE MOBILE • CHRISTMAS TABLE NAPKIN RING AND NAME PLACE

128 pages, 186 x 248mm
Full colour throughout
ISBN 1 86108 122 7

To place an order, or to obtain a complete catalogue, contact:

GMC Publications Ltd., Castle Place, 166 High Street, Lewes,
East Sussex BN7 1XU United Kingdom
Tel: 01273 488005 Fax: 01273 478606 Email: pubs@thegmcgroup.com